Growing Up in the Lord

A Study for Teenage Girls

by Jeffrey W. Hamilton

Growing Up in the Lord: A Study for Teenage Girls by
Jeffrey W. Hamilton

ISBN: 978-0-6152-1979-0

To my wonderful wife and mother of
my children.
I love you, darling!!

Table of Contents

Introduction

There is a large problem in our society. People have taken upon themselves the privilege of defining what is right and what is wrong. Their standard is their own desires and their target is our own children. Believing there is no God, they have used a standard of "feeling good" as a measure of righteousness. As a result, unrestrained sex is no longer considered sinful. Instead, the opposite is true! To teach that young people should wait until marriage to have sex is considered unreasonable and outdated.

Instead of letting the ignorant and unrighteous define the moral standard for our children, we need to make a full frontal assault on the false teachings in our public schools. God's view of sex must be taught to our children to show there is another way of looking at the world. We need to show that the Bible's teaching is relevant to today's society and that it makes sense to use the Bible as a guide.

This book is designed to teach teenage girls who have reached puberty about God's view of sex as taught in the Bible. Most of the book places heavy emphasis on the teachings found in the Bible. The early chapters concentrate on the physical aspects of womanhood. It then applies this knowledge, along with the Bible's teaching, to discuss various aspects of sex as it applies to a young woman. The later chapters cover the various ways people pervert God's gift of sex.

Throughout the book, I emphasize the point that each person is responsible for her own actions. Each thing we choose to do will have consequences, and I am very blunt about what those consequences may be. I do not accept the idea that a person "couldn't help herself." Instead, I point out the various tactics Satan uses to deceive us and ways a young woman can avoid sinning.

The wording in this book is embarrassingly plain. The plain language is the same that is used in sex education courses in the public schools, but instead of leaving the words with humanistic definitions, I define them in the light of the Scriptures. Because most of us find the topic of sex embarrassing, we look for gentle phrases to express what we would rather not say. However, for young women, the phrases have no meaning because they have no experience or it comes across as if you are trying to hide something from them. Our young women need to learn to trust us when we warn them of the dangers of unbridled sex. Indirect statements put a stumbling block in the way of that trust.

While I do describe what sex is in this book, I have purposely left out many details. I believe that a discussion of how to have a good sexual relationship should be reserved for the time just before a man and woman marry. See *Preparation for a Lifetime* by Jeffrey W. Hamilton for more information on this topic. Since the Song of Solomon is a good basis for discussing these matters, I will not cover the Song of Solomon in this book.

While gathering material for these lessons, I found that the books available in Christian bookstores were inadequate in many ways: most of the books were written before the arrival of sex education in the schools; many do not address current problems, such as homosexuality, in adequate detail; and far too many of the books used few scriptural references (the authors were probably trying not to overwhelm their students).

It is my hope that you will find the material in this book adequate to combat the false teachings that are being spread in the sex education classes of the schools today. Instead of selecting only a few verses for each lesson, I want to expose you to the wealth of information on sex that is contained within the Scriptures.

I am still working on improving the material in this book. I would welcome any comments or information that you can send my way.

All quotations are from the New King James Bible published by Thomas Nelson Publishers, 1982.

Chapter 1
What is Happening to Me?

Puberty is the time when your body begins making rapid changes from childhood into womanhood. The years of these changes are called adolescence. Adolescence literally means growing up. The exact time that puberty begins varies widely from one person to the next. On average, puberty starts around age 10 for girls, though it is not unusual for some girls to begin changing as early as age 8 or as late as age 14.

The changes to your body do not occur overnight. It takes many years for your body to fully change from a girl to a woman. On average, these changes take place over a five-year period. As with the start of the changes, the duration of the changes varies from person to person. Most of your height will be gained during your early teenage years. The majority of women reach their full adult height by age 15, though some finish as early as 12 or as late as 19. When you finish growing depends greatly on when you enter puberty.

As girls approach their teenage years a series of chemicals called estrogens are released into the blood stream. Estrogens are female hormones (male hormones are called androgens). Estrogen is manufactured in the ovaries and is released into the blood stream in large quantities about a year before you see physical changes in yourself.

The order of changes varies greatly among individual girls. Some girls first realize that they have entered puberty when they notice that their breasts have begun to grow larger. Other girls first notice puberty when they begin to grow hair under their arms and around their genitals. Still other girls first realize they have entered puberty when they suddenly gain height. For some girls the first sign of growing up is menstruation.

You will notice many changes over the next five years or so. They will not occur all at once and they will not last for all of your teenage years. Some changes will affect you deeply and some changes you will hardly notice. This, too, varies from person to person.

Increased appetite: Estrogen causes your body to grow and that growth needs additional energy. You will find yourself consuming larger quantities of food during your growth period. Just hours after your last meal, you will be looking for a snack. This is normal for a teenage girl in her growing years. Just don't let it become a permanent habit. Once your growth stops, all that extra food will be stored as fat. This is why many women gain weight as they grow older.

Mood swings: A woman's body is constantly shifting the amount of hormones flowing in her blood stream. Before you reached puberty, your hormone levels were fairly constant, but now and through much of your adult life, these hormones will fluctuate roughly on a monthly basis. During your adolescent years, the changes in your hormone levels will not be steady – in fact, one of the signs that you have completed your adolescent years is when your hormone levels take on a steady rhythm.

The changing hormones in your body regulate various functions; in particular, your organs that allow you to have children one day. When your body first develops the capability to have children, there is a period of time where the body has to learn to control the hormone levels in your blood to produce the desired effect. Early on, these hormone levels are unsteady and at times you produce too much or too little or at the wrong times. As you get older, these mechanisms calm down into a steady rhythm (though they can "hiccup" at times).

These hormones not only regulate your reproductive system, but they also affect your moods. There are going to be times during your monthly cycle when you are going to feel moody and depressed. At other times you will feel like you can take on the world. There will be times when you are irritable at the least remark, and there will be times when you feel especially attractive. This constant change will now be a part of your life for the next 40 years or so.

The worst time is usually seven to ten days before your next period. About 20 to 40 percent of all women experience cravings for sweets or salty foods, headaches, tiredness, depression, general aches, and bloating. These symptoms are referred to as PMS (premenstrual syndrome). These symptoms last up until the woman's period begins.

As Christians, we must be sober and self-controlled (I Peter 4:7; I Corinthians 9:25). A Christian woman cannot use her changing moods as an excuse to do things which are not right. Kind words are to be said at all times, not just when you feel like saying them. Bitter words are always wrong and are not excused because you are at "that time of the month."

Sleepiness: The extra energy you expend on growing will cause you to sleep a bit longer than you have in the past. It doesn't help when you find your days packed with more things to do, so that when the weekend finally comes you crash for most of the morning. It may be hard, but try to keep a regular schedule and allow yourself adequate time to rest.

Growth: Your body will rapidly change in size. For most girls, the bulk of the growth will occur about a year after you enter puberty. On average most girls experience their growth spurt between the ages of 11 and 12, though it may start as early as 9 or as late as 14. Clothes that fit you last week will suddenly be too short this week. The growth starts with your feet and hands, moves to the legs and arms, and finally extends to your trunk as you fill out and lengthen. The growth will come in spurts over the next 4 years. By the time you are 15 or 16, you will have reached your full adult height.

A difficult part about growing is adjusting to the new length. You will find yourself stumbling because your foot is now a few inches longer than it was in childhood. The length of your stride changes as well. Suddenly, you find yourself having to learn how to walk all over. As your arm lengthens, you will frequently knock things over. The glass that you see on the table is no longer as far as you remembered it being because your arm is longer. There will be several spilled drinks in your life over the next few years.

All of this clumsiness is temporary, so give yourself time to adjust to your new size. Be a little more conscious about your movements - where you put hands or where you place your feet. It is when you do things by habit that you will get yourself into trouble because you are making child-sized movements with an adult-sized body.

Even after you have reached your full adult height, your body continues to grow as it changes from a child-shaped body to a woman-shaped body. For about two years after you stop growing taller, your hips will continue to widen and your breasts will continue to develop.

Hair: Soon after puberty begins, you will notice small bumps on your skin around your groin. If you look closely you may see a fine hair growing in the center of each bump. This is the beginning of pubic hair, curly hair that grows around your genitals. As you continue to grow, hair will grow on your legs and arms. Some women even experience some fine hair growth on their upper lip. Your genes determine the amount and thickness of your hair. Except for your pubic hair, most of the hair that grows on a woman's body is fine, light hair, though some of the hair on your arms and legs may be heavier. The amount of hair a woman's body grows is totally dependent on the genes she inherited from her parents. Some women will have almost no body hair and others may have quite a bit.

Today's fashions are often designed for women with little or no body hair. As a result, many women will regularly shave the hairs on their legs and under their arms to meet these expectations.

Acne: With increased growth, your skin produces an abundance of oil – more than you had during your childhood. For many people, the glands that produce the oil become clogged with dirt or dried oil. This causes the oil to back up underneath the skin and become inflamed. The inflammation is called acne. Some teenagers develop a bad case of acne; a few lucky ones will rarely experience it. For most of you, simply make sure to thoroughly wash your face and other acne-prone areas with soap and a wash cloth. This will help to free the clogs and keep down the excess oil. For some people, even this will be inadequate and you may need to see your doctor for additional treatment. A few people who are prone to scarring will develop small scars on their face. These people will definitely want to keep tight control on their acne, since the scarring is usually permanent.

Grown women still occasionally have a pimple show up now and then. However, you will be happy to know that acne occurs less frequently after your growth stops.

Sweat: Like your oil glands, you will soon find out that your sweat glands will also be working overtime. Growing causes your body to produce excess heat. When others are pulling on extra sweaters, you may find the temperature a bit warm. As with acne, once your growth spurt stops, your body will no longer produce as much sweat.

Breasts: For most girls, the first indication that you have entered puberty is the development of your breasts. The growth usually begins between the ages of 11 and 12, though it is known for some girls to start as soon as 8 or as late as 14. Do not worry if one breast develops faster than the other. They may remain different sizes for several months, but eventually they will even out.

The development of your breasts will continue slowly for several years, often continuing through the age of 18.

Since the breasts are the most noticeable part of the female anatomy, many girls become concerned over the size of their breasts. Your final breast size is determined by the genes you inherit from your parents. Every society has an ideal of what constitutes the ideal breast size, but size from individual to individual will vary greatly, just as height varies greatly. As with most things, we need to learn to be content with what God has given us. The size of your breasts has nothing to do with your sexuality or your ability to raise children.

Menstruation: All the changes that we have talked about happen gradually over a period of several years, and the genitals are no exception. Most of the changes in a woman's body are internal. The ovaries develop and begin producing hormones and eggs. The uterus begins monthly preparations for receiving the eggs and discarding the unfertilized eggs. For the most part, you will not notice these internal changes. A more noticeable physical change to the genital area is the growth of pubic hair.

Sometime during your adolescent years, you will begin to experience a monthly flow of blood from your genitals. The blood comes from a lining formed in your uterus. We will explain this in more detail in the next chapter. The exact time that menstruation starts varies greatly among girls – anywhere between the ages of 9 and 16. Usually it occurs two years after you enter puberty. On average, most girls begin menstruating around the age of 13. If you don't experience a period by the time you are 16, you should visit the doctor to make sure everything is all right. Once you notice you have entered adolescence, you should keep a disposable pad handy. You never know when your first period (also called menarche) will begin. It usually seems to start at the most inconvenient time.

It is best during your adolescent years to use an external pad. A tampon, which is inserted in the vagina, can be used, but some girls have difficulty because of their hymen (discussed in chapter 2). Tampons must also be replaced regularly to avoid infections, such as toxic shock syndrome. As a result, most doctors recommend removing tampons at night and using an external pad instead.

Some girls notice a clear or whitish discharge from their vagina. This is a part of the normal cleansing process of the vagina and should not be of any concern unless the discharge has a strong odor (indicating the possibility of an infection). This discharge often increases in the months just before your first menarche.

If you get caught off guard and you get a blood stain on your clothing, keep in mind that rinsing the area with cold water will remove most of the blood.

At first, your periods may be irregular in timing; it will take at least a year for a regular rhythm to take place. Once the pattern is established, you will experience a blood flow for 2 to 7 days every 24 to 34 days.

Some women will experience cramps just before or during their period. This is the uterus contracting to speed up the shedding of the lining. Usually an over-the-counter pain reliever can reduce the discomfort. Some women feel the discomfort in their backs. It comes from the same source. These cramps may come even during months when your lining is not shed. Your body still goes through the motions even though all parts of your system are not working regularly.

Questions

1) When did you first notice that you had reached puberty?

2) List seven things that will change as you go through adolescence.

3) What is estrogen?

4) What causes mood swings?

5) When do many girls begin to have periods?

6) Why is it that two 12-year-olds will be at different points in their maturation even though they are the same age?

7)   What causes clumsiness in teenagers?

8)   Is there a perfect breast size?

Chapter 2
Learning About Your Body

The Female Anatomy

     We will describe the female reproductive system from the inside out, following the path of the egg through the reproductive system.

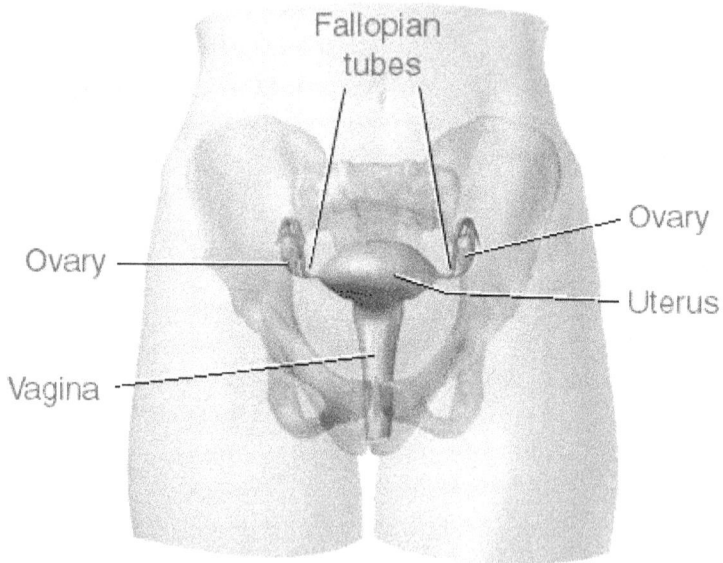

Ovaries: Each woman is born with two ovaries which are positioned in your pelvis. These oval-shaped structures produce an egg each month in response to your monthly cycle of hormones. One ovary will produce an egg one month and in the following month the other ovary will produce an egg.

     The official name for the female egg is an ovum. Each ovum is stored in compartments in your ovaries called ovarian follicles. You are born with all the ovum you will ever have, about 200,000 in each ovary. No additional eggs will be produced during your lifetime. About 400 to 500 of these eggs are released in the average woman's lifetime. Your ovaries are also the chief source of the female hormones in your body.

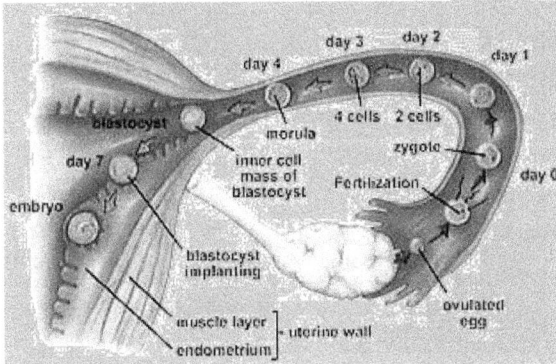

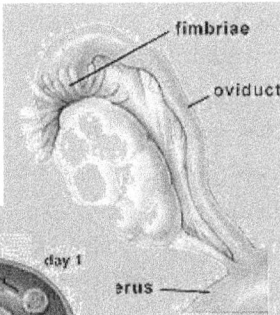

Fallopian Tubes: Near each ovary is a small, thin tube called the fallopian tube. It is about the size of a strand of hair. At the end, near the ovary, the tube fans out in finger-like extensions called fimbria. These fingers collect the egg when it is released and direct it down the fallopian tube.

It takes several days for the egg to move through the fallopian tube. If an egg becomes fertilized with male sperm, the fertilization occurs in the fallopian tube. Sometimes you will hear that a woman had a tubal pregnancy. What this means is that the fertilized egg became stuck in her fallopian tube instead of moving down into her uterus. Since the tubes are far too small to hold a developing child, she experiences sharp pain and it is likely that her tube will

burst. This is considered a medical emergency.
Fortunately, such events are rare.

Uterus: This is a muscular organ, shaped somewhat like a
pear. It has the ability to stretch many times its size and is
designed to hold a developing child. Each month, prior to
an egg being released, a blood-rich lining forms on the
interior of the uterus. If a fertilized egg becomes imbedded
in the lining, it provides the nutrients for the child to grow.
If the egg is not fertilized, the lining is sloughed off. It is
the shedding of this lining, called the endometrium, that
causes a woman's monthly blood flow.

Even though your body has matured enough to
allow a pregnancy to take place, it does not mean all the
support systems in your body have matured. Generally
these take several additional years to develop. Girls who
get pregnant before the age of 16 are at 400 times greater
risk of dying during childbirth, and they are more likely to
give birth to premature babies. A woman should wait until
she is fully developed (around the age of 18) before she
starts thinking about getting married and having children.

Cervix: A narrow opening, about the diameter of a pencil,
at the bottom of the uterus. Just before a woman delivers
her child, the doctor will measure the opening to determine
how soon the child will be born. Just before birth the
opening will widen to 10 centimeters.

Vagina: This is the passageway from the uterus to the
outside of the body. It contains many folds allowing it to
change size and stretch as needed. It is lubricated by fluids
produced by the lining of the vagina as well as by two small
glands called the Bartholins glands. The lubrication helps to

keep the vagina clean and is produced in greater abundance when you are sexually aroused. Normally, this fluid has little to no smell. If it has a strong order, it may be a sign of a yeast infection. Yeast infections are quite common, and you will need medication to get rid of it.

Hymen: This is a piece of skin that partially covers the opening to the vagina. The amount of coverage varies greatly from woman to woman. During the first time a woman has intercourse with her husband, the hymen often becomes torn. A small amount of bleeding may occur, which is sometimes referred to as proof of her virginity (Deuteronomy 22:13-21). Sometimes a woman's hymen may become torn prior to marriage due to reasons other than sex. An intact hymen is not absolute proof of a woman's virginity, and a broken hymen is not absolute proof of sexual activity.

Labia minora and labia majora: These are two sets of "lips" which protect the vaginal opening. The inner lips – the labia minor – are delicate and sensitive to the touch. The outer lips – the labia majora – are thicker and more muscular.
      During sexual arousal, these "lips" swell and form an opening to the vagina in preparation for sexual intercourse.

Clitoris: This is a small bump about the size of a pea near the top of where the two inner "lips" – the labia minora – come together. It is generally covered by a small piece of skin called a hood. When a woman becomes sexually aroused, this hood retracts exposing the clitoris. The clitoris is very sensitive to touch and is a source of pleasurable feelings during sexual intercourse. In fact, its sole function appears to be to produce sexual pleasure in a woman.

Mons veneris: This is the outer skin in the groin area that is covered with hair. It contains a layer of fatty tissue to pad the pubic bone underneath it.

Breasts: The breasts are the most noticeable part of the female anatomy. They contain milk glands, called mammary glands, surrounded by fatty tissue. Each breast contains a dark area of skin called the areola which is sensitive to touch and temperature. In the center of each areola is a nipple.

       The primary purpose of the breast is to provide milk for newborn infants. Because of the pleasurable feelings that come from being touched, they are also involved in sexual intercourse (Proverbs 5:19; Isaiah 66:11).

       Breasts come in all sorts of shapes and sizes. The shape and size of your breasts will be determined by your genes. Regardless of a breast's shape or size, they still function the same way. In many societies, girls are concerned if their breasts do not conform to their ideal of the perfect body. Interestingly, what is considered ideal varies greatly from region to region. As with all things we cannot control,

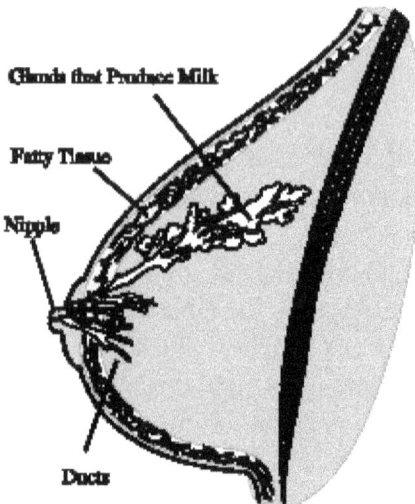

Glands that Produce Milk

Fatty Tissue

Nipple

Ducts

we need to learn to be content with what God has given us (I Timothy 6:6).

Breast sizes change constantly. The most noticeable change comes during your adolescent years as your breasts develop. However, they will change size and density slightly during your monthly cycles. This is because the varying hormones in your body affect the amount of water your body holds in reserve. Since the breast is mostly composed of fat tissue, any changes in your weight will also be noticeable in your breasts. If you become pregnant, the breasts will expand as they gear up for milk production. Finally, as you age, your skin loses its elasticity and frequently the breasts begin to sag.

Arousal

Arousal is your body's physical response to sexual stimulation. Do not confuse arousal with love; they are unrelated ideas. You will find yourself in many situations where your body will be aroused, but there is no way that you would say that you were in love.

The desire for sex is not wrong. God gave it to each of us so that it could be satisfied one day in marriage. The desire for sex is not a sin unless it spurs you to satisfy that desire in an unholy way.

Blessed is the man who endures temptation; for when he has been proved, he will receive the crown of life which the Lord has promised to those who love Him. Let no one say when he is tempted, "I am tempted by God"; for God cannot be tempted by evil, nor does He Himself tempt anyone. But each one is tempted when he is drawn away by his own desires and enticed. Then, when desire has conceived, it gives birth to sin; and sin, when it is full-grown, brings forth death. Do not be deceived, my beloved brethren.   James 1:12-16

Satan uses our desires to try to lead us into sin. He places us in situations where it seems that the only way out is to violate God's law in some manner. Don't let Satan deceive you! God has guaranteed us that He will provide a way to escape temptation that does not involve sinning.

No temptation has overtaken you except such as is common to man; but God is faithful, who will not allow you to be tempted beyond what you are able, but with the temptation will also make the way of escape, that you may be able to bear it.   I Corinthians 10:13

God didn't promise that the way out would always be easy to spot, but it is there even if we have to look hard for it. Unfortunately, when our passions are inflamed, it is difficult to think clearly. The desire for sex is very strong. Don't fool yourself into thinking that you can go part way and resist. Sometimes the best way to keep from sinning is to avoid the temptation altogether as Joseph did in **Genesis 39:1-12**.

Menstruation

Once your reproductive organs have developed enough to allow you to have children, your body goes through a monthly cycle of changes. This cycle is called the menstrual cycle. The cycle will continue until your fifties when you will enter a phase called menopause. Menopause simply means your monthly cycles have ended and you are no longer able to have children. This is why you never elderly women pregnant.

The total number of days in the menstrual cycle will vary. For younger women it tends to be more erratic and longer in duration. Once it settles down in your twenties, it typically averages about 28 days, though it can be as long as 32 days or as short as 14 days.

Under the Old Testament Law, Israelite women were considered unclean during their menstrual period. What this meant is that once her blood started to flow, a menstruating woman had to keep herself separate from other people for seven days (Leviticus 15:19-25). Anything she sat on or laid on was also considered unclean and any person touching those things would be unclean until evening. If a husband had sex with his wife during her period, he became unclean for seven days.

Even prior to the Law of Moses, people followed these laws of cleanness. When Rachel wanted to hide Laban's household idols from Laban, she sat on a saddle that had the idols underneath them and told the searching Laban that she was menstruating. Laban did not even consider asking Rachel to move from her seat (Genesis 31:32-35).

The laws of uncleanness taught the Israelites the nature of sin through physical examples. While breaking the laws were sinful, most of the events declared unclean were not sinful in and of themselves. For example, pigs are not sinful, but it was considered unclean (and a sin) to eat pork under the Law of Moses. Most of the things God selected as unclean are things we recognize today as common-sense health regulations – especially in a society that did not understand the full nature of disease and its spread. So while the primary purpose of the laws was to teach the people about the nature of sin, these same laws had a secondary effect of improving the health of the Israelite nation.

What the Israelites learned is that sin has consequences. Some of those consequences come about from choice, such as the eating of pork, but others come from natural events over which the person has no choice, such as a woman's monthly menstruation or a man's nocturnal release of semen (Leviticus 15:16-18). Since everyone experiences things they have no choice over, everyone was forced to learn these lessons. Another lesson is that sin and its consequences spread, even to those not directly involved in sin.

Some complain that God was unfair to women because they were unclean every month for seven days. They also point out that the birth of a girl required a longer period of separation than the birth of a boy (Leviticus 12:1-5). What they choose to ignore is that a man was unclean for one day each time he released semen. Since this can and often happens multiple times during a month, it was possible for a man to be unclean for more than seven days during a month. In addition, since a boy child was to be circumcised on the eighth day, this flow of blood from the operation was considered to be a part of the "payment" for the birth.

But what about the health benefits of these regulations? Since they did not have disposable sanitary napkins in those days, blood touched anything a woman sat upon. Such places can be potential breeding grounds for germs. Notice that every unclean period ended with washing of the unclean objects and the person. Israelites bathed frequently and cleaned things frequently as proscribed by their law. Isolation during times when the risk of disease was high reduced the spread of disease, keeping the general population healthier than most nations.

The laws of uncleanness passed away with the rest of the Old Testament, when Jesus died on the cross (Colossians 2:13-17). You do not have to separate yourself during your menstruation. However, the ideas of cleanliness to reduce diseases still make sense today. We still encourage women to change their pads or tampons frequently and to bathe often. It is just common-sense.

Questions

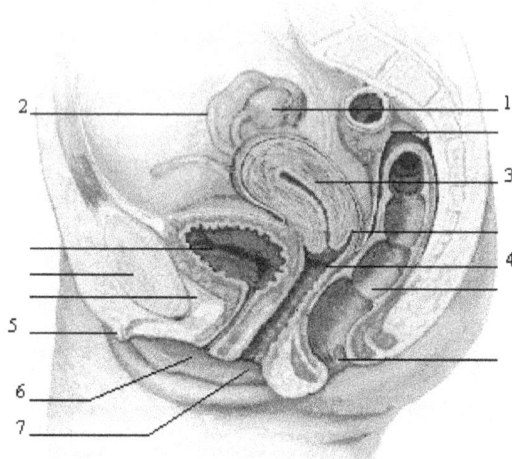

1) Using the cut-away drawing of your sex organs,
    name as many parts as you can.

    (1)   (6)
    (2)   (7)
    (3)
    (4)
    (5)

2) What causes sexual arousal? Is it a sin?

3)   Roughly how long is a menstrual cycle? What is happening during the cycle?

4)   Why was a woman unclean during her monthly blood flow?

Chapter 3
Taking Care of Your Body

Cleanliness

In **Ecclesiastes 9:8**, Solomon advises that we should always keep our clothes and bodies clean and smelling well. Even without Solomon's advice, you should be interested in making yourself presentable to the people around you.

We mentioned before that as your body expends energy to cause you to grow, you produce more oil and sweat than you have in the past. Sweat itself has little smell, but bacteria thrive in the moist environment, feeding off the oil and dead skin cells on the surface of your body. The bacteria give off a strong odor that we call body odor. You probably will not notice the smell at first, since it builds up gradually. Someone will eventually comment on the odor. As you sweat, the odor permeates your clothing and your body.

It is very simple to remove the odor. Just bathe regularly. As a child, you probably managed to get by with a bath two or three times a week. Now that you are maturing, you will find that you need to bathe daily to keep your odor level down to an acceptable range. Bathing does two things. First, it removes the excess sweat, oil, and dead skin cells, thereby removing the food source of the bacteria. Second, soap kills the bacteria that cause the odors – significantly cutting their population.

When you bathe, make sure that you scrub all of your skin. Showers are more effective than baths since the dirt rinses off and does not contact your skin again. Start your baths at the top of your head and work your way down. This keeps the loosened dirt and soap from "dirtying" areas that you have already scrubbed. As you grow, hair will form thickly around your genitals and under your arms. Simply using your wash cloth will not get the skin underneath the hair clean. Like your scalp, you need to scrub with your fingertips to remove the sweat, oil, and dead skin beneath your hair. Make sure you get all the cracks and crevices, such as behind your ears, around your genitals and between your toes.

When you clean your genital area, make sure you wash the entire vulva area. The vagina cleanses itself by producing fluids to push bacteria and dirt towards the entrance, but it is your job to clean the entrance. Make sure you rinse well as soap can be irritating to the vulva. You might also consider using a milder soap. Always wash from front to back so you do not accidently introduce germs into the vulva area.

When you sweat, most of it comes from under your arms. The hairs that grow in your armpits keep the sweat from quickly evaporating. This moist environment is ideal for growing bacteria. Use an antiperspirant to chemically reduce the amount of sweat your body produces under your arms. Another method is to use a product that discourages bacterial growth. A deodorant will not be as effective since it is basically a perfume to cover up the odors and often wears out before the day is over.

Make sure that your skin has a chance to completely dry every day. This interrupts the life cycle of the bacteria. Don't wear shoes all day long. The dark, damp environment breeds many odor-causing germs. Give your feet a chance to air out. Put on clean underwear and stockings daily so as not to reintroduce yesterday's bacteria to your freshly washed body and make sure your pelvic area is completely dry before you cover it up. Body powders can help with excess moisture around your groin and on your feet.

It was once popular to rinse the vagina with water (sometimes mixed with other chemicals, such as vinegar). It is called douching. The belief was the rinsing would cut down on the number of infections a woman may experience.

However, it is now known that douching may actually push bacteria higher up into the vagina. Also, we now know there are beneficial bacteria in the vagina which helps keep down the population of harmful bacteria. Douching too frequently will cut the population of the beneficial bacteria, giving the harmful bacteria a chance to grow out of control. So unless a doctor advises you to douche, don't.

Breast Exams

You should check your breasts regularly for lumps. Such lumps might be an early sign of breast cancer. Initially, breast cancer is painless, but it can kill you in its latter stages. It is important to catch it early, when it is more easily treated.

Breast exams should be done once a month, shortly after your period has ended. The reason for this is that just before and during your period, small lumps may temporarily appear in your breasts due to your changing hormones. The best time to examine your breasts is a few days after your period has stopped so you don't confuse the temporary lumps with more permanent ones.

You need to look and feel for two things. First, feel your entire breast for any lumps or swellings that are **different** from the way your breast felt the previous month. The fatty tissue of the breast is sometimes lumpy. Since you are the most familiar with your body, you should feel for changes within your breasts. A lump that stays the same from month-to-month is no cause for concern. Second, you should squeeze your nipples and look for any discharge or liquid from them. Unless you are pregnant or breast-feeding, your breasts should not be producing any liquid.

Dealing with Blood Flows

The products available to help with menstrual blood come in one of two forms: pads or tampons. Which one you pick depends on what you find more comfortable.

Pads are thin pieces of absorbent material that are placed on the inside of your underwear so that the pad covers your vulva. There is a sticky side on the pad to hold the pad to your underwear so it doesn't shift during the day. Pads should be changed every few hours, so keep several with you and change them each time you use the restroom. Pads come in several thicknesses. Which one you select depends on the amount of blood flow you generally experience.

Tampons are small tubes of cotton that are inserted into the vagina to absorb the blood flow. Like pads, tampons come in several sizes and absorbency rates. Depending on the size of the opening in your hymen, you may or may not be able to fit a tampon into your vagina. Also, it is very important to change the tampon regularly (every 4 to 6 hours) because it provides a good breeding area for bacteria that can cause toxic shock syndrome.

Questions

1)   What causes body odors?

2)   List at least three ways to cut down on various body odors.

3)   When and how often should you examine your breasts? What should you be looking for?

4)   How often should pads or tampons be changed?

Chapter 4
What is Sex?

Sex was Created by God

Sexual intercourse is an act between a man and a woman. The capability for having sex and the desire for sex was created by God at the very beginning.

Therefore a man shall leave his father and mother and be joined to his wife, and they shall become one flesh. Genesis 2:24

The idea that a husband and wife would become one flesh describes the joining of a man and woman in harmonious actions, including the act of sex. There are several things that we can conclude from this verse. God intended that one man would marry one woman. Within this marriage, the man and woman are expected to have sex with each other. The idea of being one excludes all others. God does not intend for a man or a woman to have multiple sex partners.

The reason God gave us sex was so that we would produce children. There are many passages where God tells mankind to "be fruitful and multiply" (**Genesis 1:28; 9:1,7; 35:11** are just a few examples). This means we are expected to have sex and to have the children that may result from engaging in sex. However, sexual intercourse is only honorable within marriage (**Hebrew 13:4**). The Greek word, translated to the English word "bed" in this verse, carries the idea of sexual intercourse and the conception of children. The word "bed" is used to represent the act that usually takes place there.

If you think for a moment, it makes sense that sex and the production of children should take place only in marriage. Children need a stable home in which to grow up.

The ideal family has a father and a mother to care for the children and to train the children in the ways of the Lord. A single parent has difficulty fulfilling two roles simultaneously. Therefore, both roles are poorly done. A single parent does not have enough time to adequately raise children according to God's word.

I should mention that not every couple is able to have children. There are many things that can go wrong with the man or the woman's body to prevent the conception of a child. The Bible mentions several couples who were barren: Abraham and Sarah, and Jacob and Rachel are two examples. Therefore, don't get the idea that every act of sex leads to the conception of a child.

Not only is sex something a husband and wife are allowed to do; it is a duty. Under the Old Law, a new husband was released from obligations, such as serving in the army, that would separate him from his wife during their first year of marriage (**Deuteronomy 24:5**). By living at home, he could concentrate on bringing happiness to his wife. Some men do not understand that women have as much a desire for sex as men do. The male desire is more visible, but this doesn't mean that the female desire is any less. In the days of the Old Testament, some men took multiple wives. God did not approve of a man being married to more than one woman, but realizing that the people were going to do it anyway, God put laws in place to make sure that each wife was at least treated fairly. In **Exodus 21:10**, if a man took another wife for some reason, he could not diminish his first wife's "marriage rights." Another way to put it is that the husband cannot withhold having sex with his original spouse. When a woman marries, she has the right to expect to have sex with her husband. Paul tells us that a reason for marriage is to prevent fornication, or sexual immorality.

Now concerning the things of which you wrote to me: It is good for a man not to touch a woman. Nevertheless, because of sexual immorality, let each man have his own wife, and let each woman have her own husband. Let the husband render to his wife the affection due her, and likewise also the wife to her husband. The wife does not have authority over her own body, but the husband does. And likewise the husband does not have authority over his own body, but the wife does. Do not deprive one another except with consent for a time, that you may give yourselves to fasting and prayer; and come together again so that Satan does not tempt you because of your lack of self-control.
I Corinthians 7:1-5

[Sexual immorality or fornication is having sex outside the realm of marriage.]

As a result, the husband must give the affection <u>due</u> his wife (and vice versa). From verse 4 we see Paul is referring to sex when he uses the word affection. Sometimes circumstances force a husband and wife to forgo sex. If that happens, Paul recommends that both the husband and the wife must agree to the abstinence and that the time of separation be limited. Otherwise, Satan will have an opportunity to tempt them to have sex with someone else.

Solomon gives some sound advice to husbands that women can learn from as well.

Drink water from your own cistern, and running water from your own well. Should your fountains be dispersed abroad, streams of water in the streets? Let them be only your own, and not for strangers with you. Let your fountain be blessed, and rejoice with the wife of your youth. As a loving deer and a graceful doe, let her breasts satisfy you at all times; and always be enraptured with her love.   **Proverbs 5:15-19**

[In the poetic language of the Bible, the act of sexual intercourse is described in terms of flowing water.]

Solomon's advice was that men and women should only
satisfy their desire (or thirst) for sex from their own well. In
other words, you should only seek satisfaction of your
sexual desires with your own husband. God does not intend
for you to have sex with any other man. As Solomon said,
why should a man disperse his water (that which satisfies his
wife's thirst for sex) in the streets? Sex between a married
couple is honorable and blessed. Therefore, enjoy sex with
your husband.

Sex is Pleasurable and Satisfying

Obviously, sex is pleasurable. If it wasn't, many
people in the world would have little or no desire to fulfill
God's command to have children. Consider the desire to eat.
It helps us to remember to fuel our bodies regularly.
Without hunger, some people would starve because they
forgot to eat. The desire for sex is a reminder to us that we
should marry and attempt to have children. However, it is
possible to go too far with the idea of satisfying our desires.
The desire to eat encourages us to fuel our bodies, but
constantly feeding ourselves results in obesity and gluttony.
Just because God gives us the desire does not give us the
right to overindulge. Far too many women overindulge their
desire for sex. They do not wait for marriage as God
commanded them. Instead of being satisfied with their
husband, they look for new sex partners. Such actions are
blatant violations of God's law. Do not let Satan lead you
away from God by indulging your desires in ways that God
never intended.

You probably have an idea about what sex is from
things that you have heard or seen. However, so that you
understand the things that we will be discussing later, let me

describe what sex is. Sexual intercourse can be divided into five phases. The first phase is the desire for sex, which is called arousal. The second phase is when the husband and wife strengthen their desires by touching and kissing each other. This phase is called foreplay. Adjustments are made in both the man and the woman's body to accomplish sexual intercourse. The woman's vagina begins producing lubricants and the man's body prepares semen. When their desire for sex has become very strong, the husband inserts his penis into his wife's vagina. This phase is called penetration. The next phase is called orgasm. Orgasm is a feeling of extreme pleasure. At this point, the man ejaculates. Semen squirts out of his penis and deep into the woman's vagina. After ejaculation, every muscle relaxes and a feeling of contentment comes over the couple. This is the final phase, which is known as afterglow.

It is important for you to understand that all phases are a part of what we call sex. Sex is not just the inserting of the penis or the release of semen into the woman. Too many teenagers engage in fondling without realizing that they are causing their bodies to begin adjustments for the next phase of sex. While the fondling is pleasurable and exciting, stopping is difficult because the body wants to complete what has been started.

Sex Outside of Marriage is Wrong

The Bible uses two words to describe wrongful sexual acts. The first word is fornication, which means any sexual act outside of or before marriage. Fornication is sometimes translated as sexual immorality. The second word is adultery. Adultery is sex between two people where at least one person is married to someone else.

Paul tells us in **I Corinthians 6:9-10** that anyone who commits fornication or adultery will not inherit the kingdom of God. We cannot be a part of God's church and participate in illicit sexual acts. Fornication and adultery are more than a sin against God; they are sins against our own bodies.

Flee sexual immorality. Every sin that a man does is outside the body, but he who commits sexual immorality sins against his own body. Or do you not know that your body is the temple of the Holy Spirit who is in you, whom you have from God, and you are not your own? For you were bought with a price; therefore glorify God in your body and in your spirit, which are God's.   I Corinthians 6:18-20

Other sins, such as thievery or lying, are committed against another person, but sexual sins affect your own life.
        Consider the story of Shechem and Dinah.

Now Dinah the daughter of Leah, whom she had borne to Jacob, went out to see the daughters of the land. And when Shechem the son of Hamor the Hivite, prince of the country, saw her, he took her and lay with her and violated her. His soul was strongly attracted to Dinah the daughter of Jacob, and he loved the young woman. So Shechem spoke to his father Hamor, saying, "Get me this young woman as a wife." And Jacob heard that he had defiled Dinah his daughter. Now his sons were with his livestock in the field; so Jacob held his peace until they came. Then Hamor the father of Shechem went out to Jacob to speak with him. And the sons of Jacob came in from the field when they heard it; and the men were grieved and very angry, because he had done a disgraceful thing in Israel by lying with Jacob's daughter, a thing which ought not to be done.   Genesis 34:1-7

[The word translated as 'defiled' or 'violated' in verse 2 carries the implication that Shechem forced himself on Dinah, possibly even raping her.]

Although Shechem later decided he loved Dinah and wanted to marry her, Dinah's brothers were angry because it was a *thing that ought not to have been done*. If Shechem truly wanted Dinah, he should have asked Jacob for her hand in marriage and then married Dinah before he took her to his bed.

Paul told early Christians in **Colossians 3:5-6** to remove fornication from their lives to avoid God's wrath. People who are not followers of God may be committing shameful sexual acts, but Christians know better than to join them in their sins. In **I Thessalonians 4:3-5**, Paul tells us to avoid fornication and to keep ourselves pure. Other people will let their passions rule their lives, but we will not be like them. We will dedicate our bodies to the honor and glory of God. (The word <u>vessel</u> is a way to describe our bodies; it is a container for our souls. The word <u>sanctification</u> means to set apart for a special purpose.) We must live and act so that other people would never associate inappropriate behavior with Christians.

But fornication and all uncleanness or covetousness, let it not even be named among you, as is fitting for saints; neither filthiness, nor foolish talking, nor coarse jesting, which are not fitting, but rather giving of thanks. For this you know, that no fornicator, unclean person, nor covetous man, who is an idolater, has any inheritance in the kingdom of Christ and God.   Ephesians 5:3-5

[Fornication is having sex with someone you are not married to. Covetousness is wanting something or someone who belongs to another person.]

Christians should not be associated with acts of fornication. Nor should they commit related sins such as making lewd gestures, using filthy language, or telling dirty jokes.

Possible Objections

Some of you who are reading this probably think that this is a cruel fate. God gives you the desire for sex and the capability to have sex, and then He turns around and tells you not to use your new ability. You need to understand that God has not forbidden sex. He has limited when you may enjoy sex (only in marriage) and with whom you may have sex (only your husband). Marriage may seem to be a long way off, but you need that time to mature. A toddler who has just learned to walk needs time to practice before he can run. In like manner, you need time to adjust to the physical and mental changes happening within you before you make a lifetime commitment to someone.

God has not set an impossible task before you. Since the world began, many women have faced the same temptations that you are now facing and they have remained pure for their future husband. Wanting to have sex, to find out what it is like, is not a desire unique to you.

No temptation has overtaken you except such as is common to man; but God is faithful, who will not allow you to be tempted beyond what you are able, but with the temptation will also make the way of escape, that you may be able to bear it. I Corinthians 10:13

[For each temptation, there is a way to avoid sinning. If you really want to please God, wait until you are married.]

Waiting is not unreasonable. To truly enjoy a sexual relationship, a man and a woman must have trust and commitment between them. Sex without love leaves you wondering if there isn't supposed to be something more to this. There is more to sex, but you can only find it when you are committed to someone for life. Sex also leads to having children. After all, God created sex to populate the world.

Raising children without a stable home is a cruel thing to do to anyone. Finally, if everyone only had sex with their spouses, all the sexually transmitted diseases (often called venereal diseases) would no longer be a problem. Venereal diseases can only be a problem when at least one of the participants in the sex act has had multiple partners.

However, don't rush into marriage just because you are anxious to have sex. Marriage is a lifetime commitment. Once you have married someone, expect to live with him for the rest of your life. You are not marrying someone to warm your bed. There are many other hours in the day that you must live with this person. Carefully consider whom you plan to marry. After you are married, enjoy all aspects of your marriage - including sex.

Questions

1)   Where did sex come from? Give two purposes for sex.

2)   Who was told to have sex?

3)   Why shouldn't a husband withhold sex from his wife?

4)   What are the five stages of sex?

5)   When is sex a sin?

6)   What is fornication? What is adultery?

7)   Give three reasons why we must wait until marriage to have sex.

8)   All sins are against God, but fornication and adultery
        are also sins against someone else. What is it?

9)   What passage of scripture tells us that lewd
        gestures, filthy language, and dirty jokes are wrong?
        Why are they wrong?

Chapter 5
What is Lust?

Lusts are <u>unlawful</u> desires. Lust is wanting something to which you have no right. Jesus explained in **Matthew 5:27-28** that lusting after a woman is the same as actually committing adultery with her. Similarly, a woman is not to lust after a man. As far as God is concerned, there is no difference between wanting to violate his laws and actually doing so. You see - your heart directs your actions. Solomon said you behave in the same manner as you think in your heart (**Proverbs 23:7**). It is the thoughts of the heart that defile us because they lead to sinful action (**Mark 7:18-23**). The things we chose to look at shows the direction in which our lives will take (**Matthew 6:22-23**). You may be looking to get as close to sin as you possibly can without committing the sin. However, it is like trying to walk on a fence between two yards. You probably can walk on it for a little way, but you will eventually slip and commit the sin.

In **Galatians 5:19-21** Paul gives a list of the works of the flesh that will keep us out of heaven. Among these works is the word lasciviousness or licentiousness, depending on the translation of your Bible. Lasciviousness means being wanton, lewd, or lustful. William Barclay described it as "a love of sin so reckless and so audacious that a man has ceased to care what God or man thinks of his actions." Lusts are wrong because you stop trying to please God.

As Christians we must remove lustful feelings from our lives. Paul warned Timothy in **II Timothy 2:22** to flee youthful lusts. Youth is a time when lusts strike the strongest and you have the least experience dealing with them. The hormones flowing through your body cause your emotions to fluctuate between extremes. There are new desires that you are now aware of, but you are still learning how to handle them. These add up to potential danger for the unwary Christian.

Instead of giving in to these desires, we must learn how to keep a tight reign on them. Peter tells us to abstain from fleshly lusts (**I Peter 2:11**). The main source of your desire for sex is from your own body. However, Satan will use a variety of tactics to try to get you to sin. John tells us in **I John 2:15-16** that Satan's deceptions come in three categories: lust of the flesh, lust of the eyes, and the pride of life. Advertising agencies are aware of these methods. They use them to "tempt" you into buying their products. Satan also uses these methods to tempt you into violating God's law.

Lusts of the flesh are those things that start out as normal desires of your body and then get out of hand. Everyone has the desire to eat, to drink, and to have sex. Satan tries to place you in situations where those desires pull you to violating God's law. For example, when Satan tempted Christ to prove he was the son of God, he asked Jesus to turn stones into bread (**Matthew 4:1-4**). At that time, Jesus was hungry. He had not eaten for 40 days. Proving who he was and getting food must have been very tempting, but Jesus did not give in.

Lusts of the eyes are those things that look good and cause you to want them when you should not. Everyone admires a beautiful flower, but it is wrong to want to take the flower out of a person's yard without permission. Similarly it is wrong to be envious of the lucky owner of the flower. Some men are very handsome, but don't let Satan tempt you into wanting to have that man for your own use or to be envious of the woman who was lucky enough to marry him.

Pride of life is the desire to be admired by others. When you want fame or fortune so badly that you would do just about anything to obtain it, Satan is given an easy target. Admiration is nice, but don't make it a goal in your life. Some women spend long hours preparing themselves so that men will find them attractive. Many women will wear form-fitting clothes or clothes that expose large portions of their skin in hopes of gaining the admiration of men. While it is not wrong to look nice, you should not center your life around such objectives. Men who are attracted by such things are not the kind of men young Christians should be hanging around with if they want to remain pleasing to God.

Let no one say when he is tempted, "I am tempted by God"; for God cannot be tempted by evil, nor does He Himself tempt anyone. But each one is tempted when he is drawn away by his own desires and enticed. Then, when desire has conceived, it gives birth to sin; and sin, when it is full-grown, brings forth death.   James 1:13-15

Everyone has desires of the body; everyone enjoys beautiful things; everyone likes admiration, but Satan uses those desires to lead us into sin. Satan will place each of you in situations where the desirable thing to do would be to violate some portion of God's law. If you give in to such desires even a single time, it becomes easier for Satan to get you to do it repeatedly. Soon you are hooked and you don't care what others think; you don't care what God thinks. Satan has your soul ensnared and all you have to look forward to is Hell. Don't take the first step. God promises us a way out of every temptation (**I Corinthians 10:13**). The way out may not be as desirable at the moment, but it is there. Consider what happened to Joseph.

Now it came to pass after these things that his master's wife cast longing eyes on Joseph, and she said, "Lie with me." But he refused and said to his master's wife, "Look, my master does not know what is with me in the house, and he has committed all that he has to my hand. There is no one greater in this house than I, nor has he kept back anything from me but you, because you are his wife. How then can I do this great wickedness, and sin against God?" So it was, as she spoke to Joseph day by day, that he did not heed her, to lie with her or to be with her. But it happened about this time, when Joseph went into the house to do his work, and none of the men of the house was inside, that she caught him

by his garment, saying, "Lie with me." But he left his garment in her
hand, and fled and ran outside.   Genesis 39:7-12

[The phrase "Lie with me" is a way of saying "Have sex with me." Sex is
usually done in bed while lying down.]

Joseph found himself alone in the house with
Potiphar's wife. She made it clear that she wanted to have
sex with him in bed and she was not going to take "no" for
an answer. What would you do if you were in Joseph's
place? It would be easy to give her what she wanted; it
would even be fun. No one would know what happened.
Besides, as your employer's wife, she could make things
miserable for you if you did not give in. On top of it all, she
is already starting to take your clothes off. What would you
do? Joseph turned and ran from the temptation. True, he
had to leave his clothes behind and flee in what today would
be called his undershorts, but he managed not to give in to
Satan's trap.

Solomon tells us not to consent to sin (**Proverbs
1:10**). That is what Joseph did and that is what each of us
must do. It won't be easy, but we do have one advantage:
God is on our side. Paul said, in **Philippians 4:13**, that he
could do all things with Jesus' help, and so can you. Ask
God for help to avoid Satan's snares of temptation
(**Matthew 6:13**). When we can't avoid Satan's traps, pray to
God for strength and guidance (**Hebrews 4:15-16**). God is
not unaware of your situation. Because of Jesus, he knows
what you are going through. Ask God for help.

It is important for us to keep ourselves pure and
unblemished by sin.

Do you not know that you are the temple of God and that the Spirit of God dwells in you? If anyone defiles the temple of God, God will destroy him. For the temple of God is holy, which temple you are. Corinthians 3:16-17

Under the Old Law, God's presence was associated with the tabernacle and the temple. However, under Christ's Law, God dwells in the heart of each Christian. Since God will have nothing to do with sin, we cannot expect God to remain in our hearts when we break His laws. Therefore, as Christians, our goal is to have nothing to do with immorality, impurity, lust, or evil desires (**Colossians 3:1-5**).

Masturbation

You may hear references to masturbation. Masturbation is when someone sexually stimulates their own body. God is silent on whether this practice is right or wrong. Too often, those who engage in masturbation fantasize about sexual relationships that are not proper. Such thoughts are lusts for unlawful relationships and are therefore sinful.

Pornography

Before we close out this chapter, I want you to be aware of one additional thing. Just because God has promised you a way out of every temptation, do not get the idea that you don't have to worry about avoiding tempting situations. Solomon asks the question in **Proverbs 6:25-28**, "Can a man take fire to his bosom, and his clothes not be burned?" If you are not near a fire, it is unlikely that you will be burnt. If you are not being tempted, you are less likely to sin. Why make Satan's job easy? Some women read pornographic material - obscene literature designed to arouse unlawful desires in the reader and to provoke lewd emotions. You know what I'm referring to: magazines like *Playgirl* or *Cosmopolitan* or books like romance novels. Many will argue that there is nothing wrong with looking at naked men. You may think you are not hurting anyone, but you are hurting yourself. When you repeatedly expose yourself to sexual temptations, it is that much easier to give in to them when Satan places you in similar situations to tempt you.

It is not just printed material. How many of the songs that you listen to talk about having sex outside of marriage? How many of the television shows that you watch feature a "one night stand" between a man and a woman buried in the story line? How often do you think you can listen to and watch these things before you start thinking that this is the way normal people behave?

Books, songs, and television too often portray men and women fondling each other as something everyone does. Fondling a young man, sometimes called petting, is a temptation for young women. The touching and stroking arouse desires in you that cannot be satisfied outside of marriage. Remember from the previous chapter that fondling prepares your body for the later stages of sex. Sure, you can stop the fondling before you go on to the next stage of sex, but it is tempting to continue for just a little while longer.

Too many women confuse the lust for sex for a sign of love. It isn't an indication of love. Many men can arouse those passions within you just by stroking you the right way. Even a woman can arouse you if she desired to do so, but you wouldn't claim it was love. Love is not something that comes from a physical act or from something you have seen or from something you have heard. Love is built on a relationship between a man and a woman that develops over time. There will come a time when you will become acquainted with a man. Soon you are the best of friends and before you know it, you can't imagine living the rest of your life without him. This is the foundation for true love. The idea that you can fall in love at first sight is completely false. You may meet someone that immediately fills you with desire, but the desire is not love. Because of the desire, you may get acquainted and eventually build up a love for each other, but love comes later, not at your first meeting.

Questions

1)   What is the difference between desire and lust?

2)   What does lasciviousness mean?

3)   What are the three devices Satan uses to tempt us to sin according to I John 2:15-16?

4)   How does Satan use our desires to lead us into sin?

5)   What did Potiphar's wife want from Joseph? Why would this have been tempting to Joseph?

6)   How did Joseph avoid giving into the temptation that Potiphar's wife offered him?

7)   Is looking at photographs of partially clad men sinful? Why or why not?

8)   Why should a Christian keep herself pure?

9)   List three examples from your own life when Satan
       tried to change your normal sexual desire into lust.

Chapter 6
Dating and Courtship

    If you haven't done so already, you will be asked to go out on a date. Dating a boy is a good time to enjoy the companionship of a male. Boys have a different perspective on life.

When you go out with different boys on a date, you have a chance to see who is available as a future marriage partner. You also have a chance to firm up in your own mind what you will be looking for in a husband.

Going out on a date gives you a chance to practice getting along with boys. Boys do not enjoy being treated the same way you treat other girls. The time you spend dating teaches you how to act around a boy.

You need to be choosy about whom you will be going out with. Some boys will understand that, because you are a Christian, there are certain things that you will not do. Some boys will enjoy the fact that they don't have to be constantly on their guard while they are with you. However, there are many boys who will use every opportunity they can find to try to get you to do things that are sinful. It is a challenge for them to see how far they can get you to go. For your own soul's sake, you are better off not dating such a boy. David warns us in **Psalms 1:1** not to associate with sinners. By continually exposing yourself to sin, you are tempted to commit a sin. That is why Paul said evil companions will corrupt your good morals (**I Corinthians 15:33**).

Another danger is when young women date older men. Boys develop on a different timetable than girls. Their growth spurt usually starts two years after the average girl's. As a result, there will be a period of time when girls your age will start looking like mature women while the boys your age still look like boys. A girl who has just started into full womanhood finds it very flattering when a handsome young man, a few years her senior, takes notice of her. Girls mistake this attention as a compliment to their maturity. All too often the attention comes about because the young man believes a young, inexperienced girl is easier to manipulate than a woman his own age.

Group dates are a good way to start out dating when you are young. If you pick your companions wisely, there will be fewer temptations in your way. A group gives you a chance to get acquainted with several people at once. You can also observe how the other girls treat their dates. Perhaps your first date won't be so awkward when it is shared with others. Some good outings with a group include bowling, playing a few rounds of putt-putt golf, canoeing, having a picnic and playing softball or volleyball, or gathering a group of young people together after church to eat ice cream.

Before you head out, spend some time thinking about what you will talk about during your date. In our society, boys tend to think and talk in terms of actions. Girls tend to think and talk about feelings. For example, if a boy and a girl were talking about an Olympic event, the boy would be interested in the score and the types of moves the athlete made. The girl would be interested in how the athlete was handling the stress and the athlete's reaction to the scoring. Neither viewpoint is good or bad. They are just different. It is those differences that make conversation on your first date so difficult. Spend some time thinking about what you would like to know about this boy you are dating.

One day, all too soon, you will begin dating to find someone suitable for a lifetime companion. If you want a companion, you must learn to be companionable. Talk about your interests and find out about his interests. Do you enjoy similar things? If the two of you don't have anything to talk about, what would marriage to such a person be like?

Make plans for the evening in advance and let your parents know where you expect to be. I know that many of you would rather keep your plans between you and your boyfriend, but you never know when an emergency may come up. Telling your parents also gives you a chance to see if your plans are respectable and appropriate. If you are too embarrassed to tell your folks, then perhaps you are planning something that a Christian ought not to do. Continue to carefully examine your motives.

Once you are out on your date, avoid changing your plans at the last minute. Don't let your emotions lead you into making a little detour to a quiet place where you can be alone with your boyfriend. It is a great temptation to go too far when there is no one around to see what you are doing. Don't go parking in the dark. Even if the first few times you don't do anything shameful, it is continually tempting to go a little farther and to get a little closer. If you want time to talk, find a well-lighted place with other people around. It will encourage you to act respectfully. Finally, don't spend time at your house or his when no one else is around. Many boys and girls find their own home comfortable and safe, so they relax their guard and do things they would not do in public. Most teenage pregnancies come about because a boy and a girl had sex at home. Somehow, people convince themselves there is no harm done if no one sees them. Don't let Satan deceive you!

In a few years, one person that you have dated will stand out among the others. You will find yourself going out with him more often than anyone else. You may even decide to stop dating anyone else. Dating only one person is called "going steady." In older generations this was known as courting. Courting a boy for a while is a logical step before he asks the big question. It gives you a little more time to finally decide if this is really the person you want to spend the rest of your life with. Just don't rush into it too soon. There are plenty of years ahead of you, so don't limit yourself to one person before you are certain this man is the one. Some girls hold on to the first boy they date out of fear there will be no others. Don't fall into this trap. There are many godly men out there looking for someone just like you to marry.

Because of the recognized dangers in dating one-on-one, some families have decided to forbid one-on-one dating except in the formal setting of courtship. In this arrangement, a boy who is interested in you must first approach your parents, asking permission to court you. If your parents approve of the boy (often asking privately if you have any interest before they give their consent), then you and the boy can spend time together, but only in monitored situations where a responsible adult can check up on the two of you. There are many advantages to this arrangement in reducing temptations, and the novelty of it in our society often makes it appealing to young men and women.

You know you are ready to go steady with a boy when you have met other boys but you prefer this man's company over everyone else. When you want to spend more time with this man and dating someone else will interfere with your time, then perhaps it is time to go steady.

However, if you feel pressure to date one person exclusively because everyone else is doing it, then you should reconsider. Some girls rush into going steady because they fear there won't be anyone else. This is another poor reason to go steady with a boy. There are hundreds of boys in the world with whom you could happily live. Don't get the idea that there is just one right person for you. Take your time. Marriage is a lifetime commitment, so don't rush the preliminary stages. Another bad reason for going steady is to hold on to a "good catch." Some girls pride themselves on having the handsomest or strongest boy in school as their exclusive boyfriend. Remember our discussion about the pride of life. Date a boy because you like him and not because you like the admiration of the other girls.

As you get comfortable with that special boy, keep in mind that there is a real temptation to do things with him that you would not do with other boys. Now is not the time to break God's law because you allow your emotions to get the better of you. Far too many teenagers allow their emotions to flare and find themselves tempted to have sex during their date.

A common excuse given for having sex on a date is that you need to find out beforehand if you are compatible or not. You could have sex with any boy. How familiar you are with having sex has nothing to do with compatibility. You should not be looking for a bed partner while you are dating. You should be looking for someone to share the rest of your life with. Once you and your boyfriend are married, you will have plenty of opportunity to learn how to have sex. There is no benefit gained by breaking God's law and having sex before you are married.

What is Love?

I've often told you in this book that various feelings and reactions are not love. Being aroused doesn't mean you are in love. Wanting to have sex with someone doesn't mean you are in love. The actual act of sex is not love, although it is called "making love" in today's slang. To understand what love really is, we need to turn over to **I Corinthians 13:1-8**.

Though I speak with the tongues of men and of angels, but have not love, I have become as sounding brass or a clanging cymbal. And though I have the gift of prophesy, and understand all mysteries and all knowledge, and though I have all faith, so that I could remove mountains, but have not love, I am nothing. And though I bestow all my goods to feed the poor, and though I give my body to be burned, but have not love, it profits me nothing.

Love suffers long and is kind; love does not envy; love does not parade itself, is not puffed up; does not behave rudely, does not seek its own, is not provoked, thinks no evil; does not rejoice in iniquity, but rejoices in the truth; bears all things, believes all things, hopes all things, endures all things. Love never fails. . .   I Corinthians 13:1-8

Paul is explaining what true love between Christians is like. The description also beautifully describes what the love between a husband and wife should be like.

When you love someone, you are willing to put up with their faults. You understand that people make mistakes and that changes take time, if they come at all. Even when he says something mean to you, you will only return kindness back. Love involves trusting the other person with all your heart. You don't envy him when he gets a big promotion at work or is honored for the things he has done in the community. Instead, you rejoice with him. A loving wife doesn't boast about how good she is and ignore her husband's accomplishments. What you do is less important to you than what he does. If you truly love someone, you won't say things that will hurt his feelings. He is more important to you than your own concerns. As a result, you will keep a tight reign on your anger and not lash out when things don't go your way.

Loving couples don't accuse each other of wickedness. Too many marriages are broken because the wife saw a woman leave the house or found some note and immediately leaped to the conclusion that her husband is having an affair. However, sometimes it is obvious that sin is taking place. When this happens, a loving wife will stand firm with the Lord. She will do everything possible to bring her husband back to the way of righteousness.

Being in love means you are optimistic. You are always hoping that things will get better. That hope helps you to get over the many rough times that you and your husband will face together.

Most of all, love doesn't fail. Planning to marry someone for a time to see if it will work out means you are not in love. You don't fall in and out of true love. Love holds on through good times and through bad times.

The Difference Between Love and Infatuation

Many people confuse infatuation with love. Each of us has a mental picture of the ideal companion. That mental picture is usually based on various physical attributes. He should be so tall, with a firm jaw, brown eyes, etc. Occasionally you meet someone who closely matches your mental ideal. You get excited and believe you have fallen in love at first sight.

This is not really love, but infatuation. You can tell the difference, because infatuation dies over time. I

guarantee that while you are "moonstruck" with a boy you won't believe that it will ever end, but it usually does. As you get to know the boy and find out about his likes and dislikes, you realize that he is not as perfect as you **imagined** him to be. The word "imagined" is the key word. You have no idea what a person is like when you first meet him. Getting to know a person takes time.

Over time an infatuation will either die or be replaced by true love. When you are truly in love, you will be aware of a person's flaws, but you have made a rational decision that you can live with them. A person who is infatuated with someone will either be totally unaware of the flaws in that person, pretend that those flaws are not there, pretend that those flaws don't matter, or believe that they can change that person over time. The last attitude can be disastrous for a relationship. People do change at times, but it is not very often and it is rarely because someone caused them to change. People change themselves because they want to make the change. When you choose a man to be your husband, you should look at who he is and not who you think you can make him into. If you do not like who he is today, you are taking a big risk thinking he will be different tomorrow. In other words, if he doesn't change before marriage, then he certainly won't change after marriage.

Talk freely with your intended companion. Some women are afraid to tell their boyfriend everything they are thinking for fear of driving him away. If your true thoughts would drive your boyfriend away, then the two of you were probably not cut out for each other. Both of you would be better off looking for someone else. Nothing could be worse than to find out you have made a lifetime commitment to someone who can't stand you.

In summary, true love is based on reality. Infatuation is based on fantasy. Before committing yourself to someone, make sure you both have a firm grip on reality.

A Small Exercise

Take a sheet of paper and write down the things that you hope to find in the man you will marry one day. Is it important that he be good looking? Does it matter to you if he is taller than you? Do you hope he is able to fix things around the house? Should he like children? How many children do you hope to raise? Give it serious consideration and don't base your answers on someone you are dating at the moment. It would be better to work on this when there is no one in particular competing for your heart. Talk to your mom or an older woman in the church about it, but make sure that it is **your** list showing what is important to you.

Try ranking your points. What is the most important? Which things would be nice, but really don't matter that much?

It may seem a little early to start thinking about whom you plan to marry. After all, marriage is still several years off. However, if you know what you are looking for, then when you finally meet the boy of your dreams, you can be confident that you are making a sound decision that you will never regret.

Have a rough list done before you start chapter 8. Through the years, continue to revise your list. The things that are important to you at 13 may seem childish at 18, so continue to think about these things.

Questions

1)   Why should girls date boys?

2)   Why should you be careful about whom you choose to date?

3)   Explain why each of the following is NOT an indication of love:
       Arousal -

       Desire for sex -

       Lust -

       Having sex -

4)   What is infatuation?

5)   Where can we read about what love is really like?

6)   Give two good reasons for going steady.

7)   Give three bad reasons for going steady.

Chapter 7
Getting (too) Close

Why do people kiss?

One day, the boy that you are dating will expect you to give him a kiss. Who knows - you may even want to give him a kiss. I wonder who started this kissing business anyway? What does it accomplish? I can't tell you everything about kissing, but I'll tell you a few facts. Kissing is a very old custom. No one knows when it started. No matter when it started, it is something men and women who really like each other are expected to do.

Kissing requires getting very close. You would only let people that you really liked and trusted to get that close to you. Therefore, kissing expresses trust in the other person. Kissing is a way of expressing tender feelings for another person. Parents kiss their children to let them know that they love them. Couples who are in love frequently kiss to express their feelings.

When should you kiss a boy? Well, don't do it just to be doing something. When you find yourself truly caring for the boy, then give him a kiss to let him know what you think. If your date hesitates or backs off, don't push it. It means that he hasn't developed the same feelings toward you yet. Some boys use kissing to make a girl believe that they really care for her. In reality, all they are interested in is encouraging them to let down their guard long enough so that they can have sex with them.

Kissing is appropriate after you have dated a boy for a few times. Give him a short kiss when he drops you off to say goodnight. Save frequent kisses for the time when you think this boy may be the one you will want to marry. Don't use kisses as a way to get a boy to like you.

Caution!

While kissing is a way of saying "I love you," there is a danger in not stopping there. As you become more familiar with a boy, there is a great temptation to go farther with him. Don't expect your date to draw the line; he is facing the same temptations. I don't mean to imply that people jump from kissing to having sex all at once. If that were the case, it would be easier to resist Satan's temptations. Instead, the temptation is always to go just a little bit farther than you did on the last date.

Ecclesiastes 3:5 tells us that there is a time to embrace and a time to refrain from embracing. You need to learn to tell the difference. Kisses, hugs, and embraces that let your boyfriend know that you care for him are fine. However, when they become passionate and whet your appetite for sex, you have gone too far. If you have any doubts about how far that is, just listen to your own body. If kissing or hugging arouses you or him, you are treading into dangerous territory. Reconsider your actions and act more chastely with your boyfriend. Paul warned Timothy in **I Timothy 5:22** to keep himself pure. You cannot continually flirt with temptations and not expect to eventually be burned by sin. Paul realized the dangers that desires can lead a person into. That is why Paul said in **I Corinthians 9:27** that he constantly kept himself under subjection.

If you allow your passions to flare and do not restrain yourself, you may find yourself committing fornication. Do you remember the definition of fornication? Fornication is having sex with a man outside of marriage. Recall that fornication is a sin that is committed against your own body (**I Corinthians 6:18-20**). We are plainly told in **I Thessalonians 4:3-6** to abstain from fornication by knowing how to hold our bodies in honor. Fornication should never be associated with Christians.

But fornication and all uncleanness or covetousness, let it not even be named among you, as is fitting for saints; neither filthiness, nor foolish talking, nor coarse jesting, which are not fitting, but rather giving of thanks. For this you know, that no fornicator, unclean person, nor

covetous man, who is an idolater, has any inheritance in the kingdom of
Christ and God.   Ephesians 5:3-5

[Filthiness is obscene or shameful speech. Foolish talking is talk that is
absurd, stupid or dull. Coarse jesting includes vulgar jokes.]

Some of you may not believe me. You may think
being aroused feels good, so you and your boyfriend will
purposely stimulate such feelings in each other. You may
convince yourself that you can stop long before things get
really serious. In the early days of your going out with him,
it was easy to stop. However, what you don't notice is that
each time you stroke each other it lasts a bit longer than it
did before. It isn't as much fun unless you get each other
aroused to a higher level of sexual desire. Most men and
women don't realize that such fondling is a part of sex. It is
called foreplay. It doesn't matter if you fondle each other
with your clothes on or not. Fondling still increases your
desire for sexual release and prepares your body for having
sexual intercourse. Already you have entered Satan's realm
of sin since you are furthering your desire to have sex
outside of marriage. Fornication is wrong. It is a sin.
Wanting to commit fornication is also a sin. This sin is
called lust.

Sometimes a boy will believe and imply that you
owe him for the expenses he has incurred in dating you.
Some girls actually buy that line and figure a little
stimulating playing around will not do any harm. Your
body is yours alone to possess. If you plan to marry, your
body should be saved for your future husband when the
bonds of marriage have been put into place (**Song of
Solomon 8:10-12**). You don't owe anyone sexual
gratification. The very idea puts the actions on the level of
a person paying a prostitute for sexual "services."

Once you are aroused, your body begins producing lubricants for eventual intercourse. Now you have a problem: your body wants to continue so it can complete what was started. *Don't let yourself get anywhere close to this point!* Go home as quickly as you can, even if it is earlier than you had planned. Learn your lesson and behave more chastely from now on. If your boyfriend asks, explain to him that the fondling is too stimulating. Admit you don't feel you can restrain yourself if you continue much longer. If he is a decent boy, he should understand. He probably was struggling with the same problem.

Some will not heed their own bodies' warnings. They will continue to stroke and fondle each other often to the point of orgasm. You and your boyfriend can stimulate each other to a sexual frenzy without actual intercourse.

There are many misconceptions about how far you can go without going too far. Many couples gauge their love for each other by how far they can stimulate passions in each other. Love has nothing to do with sexual lust. Remember, one aspect of true love is that it thinks no evil. Fondling each other to the point where you can't think of anything else but completing the act of sex, although you are not married, is a sin. If you truly loved someone, you would not subject him to such a sin.

Many people feel that as long as a pregnancy does not occur, their actions are justified. We have already shown the fallacy of this idea, but I would like to go over a few ways people excuse themselves for going too far.

"If I don't give him what he wants, he'll dump me."

If he is only seeing you because he thinks he can have sex with you, then it would be better to find a decent boyfriend. No boyfriend at all is better than one who lures you into sin.

"If we keep our underwear on, it's all right."

The problem here is: what will prevent you from going further later? With so little clothing on your bodies, it is very tempting to just go a little bit further. Of course, we still have the fact that we are dealing with the sin of lasciviousness (lust for sex outside of marriage). Just because you avoid copulation doesn't mean that you are sinless.

You may not realize it, but even clothed, it is still possible for a girl to get pregnant. Many cases have been documented where girls found themselves with child and never had intercourse with a boy. Pregnancy will occur if one of his sperm unites with your egg. It doesn't matter how the sperm gets into your vagina. Couples who excite themselves to the point that the boy ejaculates usually continue to fondle each other afterwards. A finger, with even a small amount of semen on it, in your vagina, is sufficient to cause pregnancy. In addition, just because it didn't happen the previous time does not guarantee that it won't happen the next time.

Another problem is that underwear is a very poor barrier to semen; it soaks right through. Since couples who are engaged in fondling each other are usually pressed close together, it is very likely that the boy's semen will soak into the girl's panties. Even if the semen doesn't immediately reach the vagina, it could be accidentally pushed there later.

Finally, if a boy does ejaculate, there is enough force there to squirt it through your underwear and into the front part of your vagina.

"We played around so long, he is too excited to stop."

You don't owe any man sex outside of marriage. If your mutual actions have gotten him highly aroused, it is better to stop than to press on to further sin. A boy's body has the ability to release excess semen without having to have intercourse. The excuse that he has to complete what was started is just a desire to fulfill his lust.

"He'll withdraw before he ejaculates."

The attempt here is to have sex, but avoid any pregnancy. From God's viewpoint, you are still committing fornication. Fornication is having sex when you are not married. It doesn't matter whether pregnancy results or not. The reason most couples don't want a pregnancy to occur is that it would be positive proof that they had been sinning. As with other sins, it is nearly impossible to commit the act and avoid the consequences. The reason God gave us sex is so that we can produce children. Every time you engage in sex, there is a strong probability that a pregnancy will result. For married couples trying to have a baby, the odds are one in five that a pregnancy will occur.

As you approach the point of orgasm, your muscles become very tense with pleasure. As the boy approaches the point of release, he will find it difficult to withdraw his penis quickly due to the tension. Too many boys cut the time too close and accidentally ejaculate in the girl's vagina anyway. Once the semen enters your body, there is no way to get it back. Some girls falsely think that if they flush their vagina after sex that it will prevent pregnancy. Usually, all they accomplish is to push some sperm further toward their uterus.

Even if he does manage to withdraw in time, you still face the danger of accidentally pushing the semen into the vagina afterwards. You also face the danger of picking up a disease. There are several diseases that are easily picked up during sexual intercourse. Even if he withdraws before ejaculating sperm, the skin-to-skin contact during intercourse can and often does transmit a disease. Most sexually transmitted diseases do not have visible symptoms, but they can cause severe internal damage to your body. For example, chlamydia and gonorrhea can cause you to lose your ability to have children if the disease is not caught quickly. Venereal warts is strongly associated with cancer of the cervix. Perhaps the greatest danger of some of these diseases is that noticeable symptoms take years to develop.

Finally, it really doesn't matter if he didn't ejaculate into your vagina. The male body produces lubricating fluid when he is aroused, just as your body does. That fluid usually contains small amounts of sperm. It is true that there isn't a whole lot, but all you need is one sperm to reach the egg. I've personally met young teenagers who found this out the hard way. Don't fool yourself into believing that it won't happen to you.

"We'll only do it when it is safe."

The hard part is knowing when it is safe. The menstrual cycle is composed of four phases. The first phase is the preparation of the uterus for the receiving of a fertilized egg. A lining of blood vessels build up on the walls of the uterus. The length of this phase varies greatly, but it is about seven days long. The second phase is the release of an egg. It is during this phase that a woman can become pregnant. The third phase is the time the egg travels down to the womb. If it was fertilized with the sperm from a man, it will plant itself in the lining of the womb and the start of a nine-month pregnancy begins. If the egg was not fertilized, then the body moves into the fourth phase, which is the shedding of the old lining. This fourth phase is commonly called a woman's "period." A woman's egg is released about 14 days before her next menstrual period and can be fertilized for 24 hours after its release. While the average menstrual cycle is 21 to 28 days, few women have absolutely regular periods, especially during adolescence. Since it is difficult to accurately predict when the next period will begin, a woman cannot accurately predict when she is most fertile.

In addition, a man's sperm survives up to six days in a woman's uterus. So even if you don't have sex on the day you ovulate, you can still can become pregnant.

28 Day Menstrual Cycle

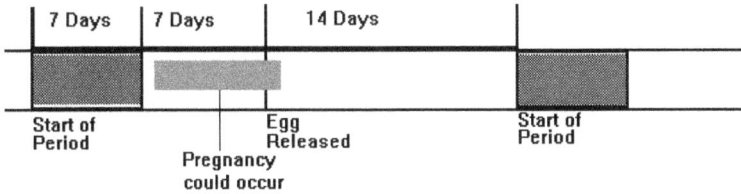

| 7 Days | 7 Days | 14 Days |

Start of
Period

Egg
Released

Pregnancy
could occur

Start of
Period

21 Day Menstrual Cycle

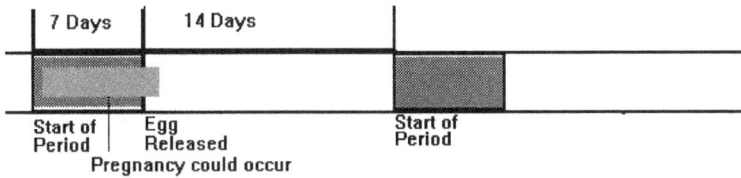

| 7 Days | 14 Days |

Start of
Period

Egg
Released

Start of
Period

Pregnancy could occur

Some couples try to avoid pregnancies by only having sex during the woman's menstrual period. Suppose a woman's cycle is short this month (only 21 days). A period usually lasts 2 to 7 days. If a couple has sex near the end of the woman's period, it is possible for her to become pregnant. We should also note that God considered having sex during a woman's menstrual period an act that defiles a nation (Leviticus 18:3, 19, 24-27). Under Mosaical Law, purposely having sex during a woman's period was punishable by exile (Leviticus 20:18).

Since a woman's body functions on a monthly cycle, there are times when you are more interested in sex than at other times. A woman's peak interest in sex coincides with the time of the month when she is most likely to become pregnant. (It makes sense that God created you that way.) This increases the possibility of pregnancies.

To sum all this up, there is no reliable way to decide when a couple can have sex and not wind up with a pregnancy. Trying to have sex during a "safe" period is simply trying to commit a sin and avoid its consequences. Every thief tries to steal when he is not likely to be caught. However, whether a thief is caught or not does not remove the fact that he has sinned before God.

"We'll practice safe sex."

You are assuming a condom will be handy when the two of you get into the mood to have sex. Too often the decision to have sex is done at the spur of the moment. Few men are interested in stopping the foreplay so that they can run down to the neighborhood drug store to buy a condom. By the time he gets back, the magic of the moment is usually gone. Even if a condom is handy, many men don't want to interrupt the foreplay to put one on. I doubt that very many of you would keep one on hand, since your parents may find it and ask embarrassing, and very justified, questions.

Another problem is that condoms have a 7% failure rate - usually due to small pin holes or weak spots that tear during sex. How would you like to eat at a restaurant where you only have a 7% chance of getting food poisoning? Yet, somehow people fool themselves into believing that using a condom makes sex "safe." In some schools, boys are encouraged to carry a condom in their wallet, just in case. Ignoring the implication that he is being encouraged to plan on sinning, the heat from his body will cause the condom to decay more rapidly than on a shelf. As a result, condoms stored in a wallet have a failure rate higher than the usual 7%. Even if a pregnancy never occurs, it doesn't make you safe from God's wrath.

Some men forget to remove the condom soon after sex. Once the penis returns to its flaccid state, the condom easily slips off, allowing semen to enter the vagina accidentally. There is also a chance that the man improperly puts the condom on which increases the likelihood that it will tear.

Taken together, couples who use condoms still face a 20% probability of an unwanted pregnancy. Why take the unnecessary risk in this life and in the life to come?

Pregnancy is only one risk in having sex. It is possible to contract some serious diseases while engaging in sex with a partner who has been engaging in sex with other people. Since many of these diseases are spread by direct skin contact, the use of a condom may reduce the possibility of contracting a disease. However, a condom cannot totally eliminate the spread os disease because it must cover all areas of contact. If a condom does not fully cover the man's penis or if it rolls up during intercourse, even part way, the possibility of transmitting a disease exists. In addition, some disease, such as herpes, does not require contact with the skin of the penis to be transmitted.

Similarly, some girls think there is no problem so long as they take birth control pills. The biggest problem is that taking these pills means you are planning to have sex, and sex outside of marriage is always wrong. In addition, birth control pills do not protect you at all from sexually-transmitted diseases. The pill only reduces the likelihood that you will become pregnant.

"He says that if I truly love him, then I would show it."

If he really loved you, he would not be asking you to sin with him. True love wants the best for the other person.

Besides, the physical actions of intercourse have little to do with the emotional feelings of love. Most boys can perform sexual intercourse with little or no emotional attachment to the girl. In a survey of 1,000 boys, 70 percent of the boys believed it was okay to lie to a girl about being in love with her in order to get her to have sex. Instead of trying to prove your love for him by committing fornication, have him prove his love for you by being willing to commit himself to marriage and then waiting for marriage before engaging in sex.

"We plan to get married."

A man will say that he would like to marry the woman, but he is not ready to make a commitment. The marriage is viewed as only a formality that can be put off to a later date. The problem is that if the man is unwilling to take the vows of marriage with you, then he is leaving his options open to leave you one day. Yet many women will view this vague possibility as firm commitment and begin to engage in sexual intercourse.

A similar error is made when a man asks to marry the woman, but no date is set. This is not a true engagement, yet it seems enough of a commitment to move in with each other and engage in sexual activity.

Even if a couple is engaged "with a ring and a date," it does not justify committing fornication. A marriage takes place when vows are exchanged before God (Malachi 2:14). Without those vows, a man may not feel any obligation to a woman with whom he happens to sleep. Nothing prevents him from walking away, other than a small amount of guilt that is quickly forgotten. Sex only belongs within a marriage. Sex outside of marriage – even during the engagement period – is fornication. Do not let a man eager for sex deceive you. You do not have a commitment until you are wed.

Questions

1) What does a kiss mean?

2) What does it mean to keep your body under subjection (I Corinthians 9:27)?

3) Why is it hard to stop fondling?

4) Name some ways we know we are going too far in our relationship with a boy.

5) Many girls try to experience the excitement of sin without going too far. What is wrong with this attitude?

6) What do people mean by "safe sex"? Is sex outside of marriage ever safe? Why or why not?

7) What ways have you heard girls using to try to experience sex without getting pregnant or picking up a venereal disease? Would they truly work? Would God approve of them?

8)   What are some lines you've heard boys use to encourage a girl to have sex with him? What would be a good response to those lines?

Chapter 8
Who are You Going to Marry?

Why Get Married?

When you look around at today's world, you see people living in many different situations. Some are married, some live alone, and still others live with a partner but are unmarried. Which should you do?

Marriage was instituted by God at the very beginning of the world (**Genesis 2:22-24**). In other words, it has God's blessing and approval. God recognized that it was not good for a man to be alone, so he created woman. Therefore, the primary purpose of marriage is to have a lifetime companion. It is fun to go and do things on your own, but it is much more enjoyable when there is someone to share the experience with you. Solomon recommends that men enjoy life with their wives (**Ecclesiastes 9:9**).

Right now, you are probably living at home. Your parents, brothers, and sisters have been providing companionship since the day that you were born. However, in the future, you will need to strike out on your own. You don't realize how much you depended on your own family for companionship until you find there is no one to turn to when you are away from home. Don't get me wrong. Some people enjoy being independent. Some enjoy it so much that they never bother to get married. However, I suspect that most of you will prefer to have a husband one day.

Being married is honorable (**Hebrews 13:4**). After all, it is approved by God. Only a false teacher would forbid a person from ever getting married (**I Timothy 4:1-3**).

Without marriage, there would be a lot more sin going on in the world. Sex is only approved by God between married couples. Without marriage, many people would be guilty of fornication. Each of you has a strong desire for sex that will continue to increase into your early twenties. Marriage is the proper way to have an opportunity to satisfy that desire (**I Corinthians 7:1-9**).

When you get married, your husband has the right to expect you to have sex with him regularly. Similarly, you have the right to ask your husband for sex as often as you need it to satisfy your desires. It would be wrong for either of you to withhold sex from the other, except if you both had agreed to stop for a short time. Some married couples withhold sex from each other to hurt their partner when things do not go their way. However, God does not want us to settle our differences in this manner. Withholding sex tempts your spouse to find sexual satisfaction elsewhere. You do not want to be guilty of placing a stumbling block in front of a person.

If you feel you can't live without sex, then you should get married. If you don't know how to be a lifetime companion to someone, then you need to learn quickly, because only in marriage does God allow Christians to have sex.

Who Should I Marry?

I hope that you have been thinking about this question since I assigned it two chapters ago. Deciding whom you plan to marry is a tough decision. It is a very important decision. Many of your friends will rush into marriage with just about any boy they believe that they love. To them, if it doesn't work out, they can always get a divorce and marry someone else. What they don't realize is that divorces are heart rending and expensive.

As Christians, you don't have the option of divorcing someone because you feel like it. Christians marry for life (**Romans 7:2-3**). There are some Christians who have been divorced, but it should be a rare occurrence. A divorce means that at least one partner in a marriage has committed a sin. A person cannot remain in sin and be pleasing to God (**I John 1:5-2:6**). The only reason that God has ever allowed for divorce is if one partner in a marriage has been guilty of having sex with someone else (**Matthew 19:8-10**). Even then, a person is <u>not required</u> to end the marriage. God only permits divorce when the people involved are too hardhearted to work out the problem. This allowance by God is not a license to have sex with someone else whenever you want to get out of a marriage. God said He will hold you responsible for adultery. If you ever marry another person, the person who marries you will also be guilty of adultery.

You can see that choosing a husband is a very important decision. You will be stuck with your choice for the rest of your life, so think long and hard about whom it is going to be. Each woman is only permitted one husband (**I Corinthians 7:2**).

Pick out the characteristics of your future husband before you have any particular person in mind. If there already is someone special in your life, you will tend to slant everything toward that man. Think about what is really important to you:

Are there things that you like to do that your
future spouse should like as well? If you
really like snow skiing, are you going to be
happy with a man who is miserable when the
temperature drops below 50 degrees?

Do you both have the same ideas about how
many children you would like to have? How
soon do you want to start a family?

Do you have plans to work outside the
home? Is he comfortable with that decision?
Does he expect you to work another job
when the children are small?

Do you care about how neatly your husband
will keep your house? If you are curious,
consider how he keeps his own room at
home. It will give you some idea about his
standards of neatness.

Are you going to share in the household
chores? Who is going to wash dishes after
dinner? Who is going to mow the lawn? Who
is responsible for repairing the leaking pipe?

The most important thing to consider is your
religion. Is your husband going to encourage to you to be a
better Christian, or is he going to moan and groan about
having to go to church on Sunday morning? Consider this
point carefully. Some men will regularly attend services with
you while they think you are interested in marrying them.
After marriage, they often find excuses to stop going. Did

he faithfully attend services before you met? If you have to go out of town, does he continue to go to worship without you? Does he enjoy studying the Scriptures? Can you study together? Are you comfortable praying with him? Consider the words of Paul:

Do not be unequally yoked together with unbelievers. For what fellowship has righteousness with lawlessness? And what communion has light with darkness? And what accord has Christ with Belial? Or what part has a believer with an unbeliever? And what agreement has the temple of God with idols? For you are the temple of the living God. As God has said: "I will dwell in them and walk among them. I will be their God, and they shall be My people." Therefore "Come out from among them and be separate," says the Lord. "Do not touch what is unclean, and I will receive you. I will be a Father to you, and you shall be My sons and daughters," says the Lord Almighty. Therefore, having these promises, beloved, let us cleanse ourselves from all filthiness of the flesh and spirit, perfecting holiness in the fear of God.   II Corinthians 6:14-7:1

Paul was addressing the more general responsibility of not compromising your faith. However, the most important contract you will make with another person on this earth will be the one you make with your husband. In this important binding of two people, it is very important that they be equally yoked.

What you believe is also important. You will have for unending battles if he wants to go to his church and you to your own. Marriage is a time for doing things together and that includes worshiping God. Even if you could arrive at a compromise in the early part of your marriage, what will you do when you begin to raise a family? Are the children going to be raised in your faith or his?

Save yourself future heartaches and marry a faithful Christian who believes as you do. Jesus prayed that his disciples be one, just as God and Jesus were one (**John**

17:20-23). Make sure that oneness fills your lives as husband and wife.

After saying all of this, I must warn you not to go overboard and start looking for the absolute perfect companion. Everyone you meet will have some "flaws;" the question is how important are those things to your (and his) future happiness. You have lived a long time with your parents, brothers, and sisters. You did not get to pick them, yet you have managed to live with them for many years. In some cultures, like in the days of Abraham, a man did not get to choose his wife. The parents arranged the marriage. In Isaac's case, Abraham's servant was sent to select Isaac's wife from distant relations whom Isaac never met. Even in these circumstances, a woman lived with her husband for their entire life.

Once you are married, you must <u>stop</u> looking for a better mate. It will be harder than you think. After spending years trying to decide whom you would rather live with, you will find that it is hard to drop the habit. Many marriages have been broken and affairs started because a woman thought she found someone even better than her current husband. There are hundreds, maybe even thousands of men that you could have married and with whom you could have happily lived. However, once you have made the commitment, you must do everything in your power to uphold your end of the deal. It may seem that someone else would make you a better husband, but that is probably because you haven't been living in the same house with him. Instead of wishing for what might have been, be prepared to throw all your energies into making your marriage prosper.

Of course, it is easier to live with some people than with others. That is why it is so important for you to make a careful decision. A story is told of a man who was trying to illustrate this very point to his student. He had the boy climb up on a table and try to pull him up to the boy's level. The boy struggled earnestly, but he was unable to budge the man. The man then calmly pulled the boy off the table with one hand. It was very easy to do. "That," he said, "is why you must look for a Christian wife." Yes, you could marry a non-Christian in hopes that one day you can influence him to become a Christian. However, that non-Christian husband will have an easier time influencing you to give up your faith, if he so desires, than you will have of turning him toward Christ. Paul warns, in **I Corinthians 15:33**, that bad companions will corrupt your good morals. Abraham understood this problem. He refused to find a wife for his son Isaac among the non-believing people around him. Instead, he sent his servant back to his own people to find a wife for his son (**Genesis 24:1-4**).

Can you understand now why God forbade the Israelites to marry non-Jewish people (**Nehemiah 13:23-27**)? Those marriages led more Israelites away from God than any other factor we can find in the Old Testament. For a similar reason, God told the Corinthian widows, in **I Corinthians 7:39**, to only marry another Christian. If it makes sense the second time around, doesn't it make good advice the first time? Don't become unequally yoked to a nonbeliever (**II Corinthians 6:14-18**).

When Should I Marry?

Take your time and don't rush this important decision. First, let your body finish maturing and wait until your hormones settle down into a steady rhythm. Don't marry out of passion. Strong sexual desire for someone lasts for only a short time. There needs to be something else –

something stronger and more enduring to build a lifetime relationship upon. When you find the right person, the passion will be there, but there will be another feeling there as well. When you find yourself caring for a man, thinking of him as someone important in your life; when you find that he is your best friend, someone you trust with your deepest thoughts and with whom you thoroughly enjoy talking; then, maybe, just maybe, you have fallen in love. Take time to read **I Corinthians 13:1-8** and see if these points apply to your relationship with this man. Only then consider spending the rest of your life with him. Get married and enjoy the husband of your youth for the rest of your lives together.

Questions

1)   Why should a woman get married? (Give at least three reasons.)

2)   Is sex optional in a marriage relationship? Why or why not? (Consult I Corinthians 7:1-9 before answering.)

3)   What is God's opinion on divorce?

4)   When a Christian marries, how long is that marriage to last?

5)   What is the most important thing that you will be looking for in potential husband?

6)   Should you look for the absolutely perfect husband? Why or why not?

7)   How do you know when you have found the man
        with whom to spend the rest of your life?

Chapter 9
Dancing

Dancing in the Bible

We will divide the discussion of dancing in the Bible into two sections. The first section will include those Scriptures where dancing is spoken of in a favorable setting. The second section is where dancing is associated with wickedness. We will note the things that are similar within each section and the things that make each section different. Once we understand the Bible's view of dancing, we will compare modern dancing to these two sections to see where it fits. As you read the verses in the next two sections, take a piece of paper and answer the following questions for each verse:

1. Who danced?
2. With whom did they dance?
3. Why did they dance?
4. Was the dance similar to today's dances?

Favorable

Dancing was used as an act of celebration. For example, when the Israelites safely crossed the Red Sea and the Egyptian army was destroyed, Miriam and the other Israelite women danced for joy on the banks of the Red Sea (**Exodus 15:20-21**). Other Scriptures that illustrate celebrations by dancing are **Judges 11:34**, **I Samuel 18:6-7**, and **Luke 15:25**.

Similarly, dancing is a way to express happiness. Jeremiah said that when joy left the people, dancing would cease (**Lamentations 5:15**). There was dancing at the father's house when the prodigal son returned (**Luke 15:25**). Other Scriptures that talk about dancing for joy are **Psalms 30:11** and **Jeremiah 31:4,13**.

Since praising God is a form of celebrating and expressing happiness, dancing was used by the Israelites to praise God. David danced before the ark of God as he attempted to bring the ark to Jerusalem (**II Samuel 6:14-23** and **I Chronicles 15:29**). The psalmist in **Psalms 149:3** recommended praising God with dance.

Look over the paper you wrote. Do you notice some similarities between these dances? In each case, the people dancing either danced alone or with members of their own sex. Not one of these dances involved men dancing with women. Each dance was an expression of the dancer's feelings. The dances were not done for exercise or to entertain other people.

Unfavorable

Teaching one's children to dance was an attribute of idle wealth in **Job 21:11-15**. By implication, people busy with the Lord's work have better things to do with their time and money.

When a raiding party captured some Israelite women, they celebrated with a drunken feast, which included dancing (**I Samuel 30:16**). The idol worship that the Israelites engaged in while Moses was on Mt. Sinai also included dancing and drinking (**Exodus 32:6, 19**).

In the list of the works of the flesh, in **Galatians 5:19-21**, Paul mentions revelries. Revelries are wild parties that usually include drinking and dancing.

Herodius's daughter danced to entertain her stepfather and his guests. The dancing so pleased her stepfather that he rashly promised her anything she wanted, up to half his kingdom (**Matthew 14:6-8** and **Mark 6:22-23**). Because of this dance, John the baptizer lost his life.

In these dances we again notice some similarities. The dances were often done as a form of entertainment. They were also done as part of celebrations, but they celebrated the works of man instead of God. These celebrations were often associated with drunkenness and wild parties.

Modern Dances

Under which category would you place today's dances? Today's dances are usually done as a form of entertainment. Dances are rarely done to celebrate (except short ones done by football players after scoring a touchdown). Modern dances also feature a sexual theme. Don't look so dumbfounded! Of course sexual arousal is a major reason people dance today. Think about it. Do you think it is normal for a man to dance with a man? Why not? It is because dancing is sexually stimulating, and we realize that it is improper for a man to arouse another man. To do so is an indication that the men involved are homosexuals. If you are having difficulty understanding the sexual overtones of modern dance, ask yourself "Would you like to see your mother doing a slow dance with a stranger?" Most of us would immediately answer NO! Such actions would suggest an affection between the two people - an affection that should only be shown between a husband and his wife.

Consider the movements involved in today's dances. The slow dances involve a man closely holding a woman against his body, which we know is very stimulating. The wilder, fast dances contain movements like thrusting your hips backwards and forwards. These movements are imitations of the act of sex between a man and a woman. Few people would engage in sex in full public view. Yet society seems to feel it is all right for a man and woman to pantomime sex in public.

If dancing is just an innocent pastime, why are there chaperons at all of your school dances? The chaperons are there to make sure that things do not get out of hand. When boys' and girls' passions are aroused, they will do many things that they ought not to do. Boys and girls to sneak in drinks or to sneak out for a quiet rendezvous to relieve their sexual lust is not unheard of.

Have you ever wondered why most adult dances take place in bars and in other places where alcohol is served? Most people want to have some drinks to make them feel more comfortable dancing with a stranger. You see, one effect of alcohol is to lower inhibitions. People will do things under the influence of alcohol that they would never do when they are sober. That is why there are so many exhortations in the Scriptures for Christians to remain sober. It is hard enough to fight off Satan's temptations, but to lower our resistance with chemicals just makes Satan's job easier.

Look at the advertisements for the theater dances in your local paper. Have you ever noticed how scantily clad the dancers are? Even the little clothing that they do wear is so tight that you can see every feature of the person's body, including the genitals. I submit to your consideration that the dancers dress like this because they know that their audience is aroused by such displays. If you want to make money, sex sells.

Now, what are your thoughts? Why do people that you know dance today? Do you think that sex plays a major role, even if it is not acknowledged by the people involved? Some people claim that they only dance for the exercise. It is true that vigorous dancing is good exercise, but are there not other ways that accomplish the same goal? Why are these other methods of exercise not as popular as dancing?

Questions

1)   Fill in the following table:

Verse	Who danced?	With whom did they dance?	Why were they dancing?	Was it like modern dances?
Exodus 15:20-21				
I Samuel 18:6-7				
Psalms 30:11				
II Samuel 6:14-23				
Job 21:11-12				
Exodus 32:6,19				

2)   What is the purpose of today's dances? (Justify your answer)

3)   Should a Christian participate in modern dances?
        Why or why not?

Chapter 10
Proper Attire

Modest Apparel

Therefore I desire that the men pray everywhere, lifting up holy hands, without wrath and doubting; in like manner also, that the women adorn themselves in modest apparel, with propriety and moderation, not with braided hair or gold or pearls or costly clothing, but, which is proper for women professing godliness, with good works.   I Timothy 2:8-10

This commandment was specifically written for women, but principles taught in this passage can be applied to men as well as women. Christians are to be modestly attired. Few people dispute this. However, when we try to define what modesty is, we are faced with many different opinions. The Amish (a religious sect that wears clothing styles dating back to the late 1600's) debate whether suspenders are modest or immodest. Some say they are modest; some say they should not be worn; still others say that only suspenders that form a "Y" in the back are modest, the "X" style is immodest.

So how do we figure out what is modest? The latest fashions are constantly changing. In the late 1800's it was immodest for a

woman to show her ankles. Therefore, women wore long dresses and high top boots. Today, no one thinks twice if a woman's ankles show. A woman wearing high top boots and a long full skirt would have many people staring at her as she walked down Main Street. Even if we restrict ourselves to the current fashions, there are some outfits that everyone would agree are definitely modest and others that are definitely immodest. However, we can't rely on popular opinion to totally define modesty. It shifts too much and often allows things that would offend most of our tastes as Christians. What we need is an unchanging yardstick to learn if an outfit is modest. That yardstick will be the Bible.

The problem of modesty originated in **Genesis 3**. Before sin entered the world, both Adam and Eve were naked. This was neither wrong nor shameful because that is the way God created them (**Genesis 2:25**). Their nakedness expressed their innocence of sin. This state did not last. When Adam and Eve sinned, they became aware of their nakedness and tried to cover themselves (**Genesis 3:7**). Their first attempt was to sew fig leaves into coverings. The Hebrew word for the garment is *chargorah*, which means a garment that covers the mid-section of the body, tied about the waist. The same word is translated in other passages as a girdle or a belt. Adam and Eve's attempt was unsuccessful, because they still considered themselves naked. When God visited them in the Garden, they hid themselves because they were naked (**Genesis 3:10**). After God issued the punishments to Adam and Eve for their sin, he took animal skins and made tunics for the man and woman (**Genesis 3:21**). The Hebrew word for tunic is *kethoneth*, which describes a shirt that reaches to the knees.

We can now define nakedness. Nakedness is the exposure of the sexual organs. Any clothing that allows a view of these parts is considered equivalent to being naked. In **Job 22:6**, the Bible talks about stripping the naked of their clothing. In other words, it is possible to be naked and clothed at the same time. The phrasing implies a person who is thinly clad (wearing clothing whose material is transparent), leaving people with no doubts about what exists underneath the clothing. Another way a person can be naked is by wearing clothing that does not completely cover in all situations. God told the Israelites not to place the altar up where the priest would have to climb steps to reach it (**Exodus 20:26**). As the priest walked up the steps, there would be the possibility of the worshiper at the base of the steps seeing underneath the priest's garments. As an additional precaution, the priest's garments included short trousers that went from the waist to the thighs to cover their nakedness (**Exodus 28:42-43**). For a woman, the exposure of her breasts or her groin region would be considered nakedness (**Ezekiel 16:7**).

Therefore, any clothing that does not cover your sexual organs in all positions would be improper for a Christian to wear. For women, this would mean the region from the shoulders to the thighs must be covered. String bikinis, bikini briefs and shorts that are split on the sides up to the waist would not be adequate coverage. Clothing made out of very thin material or loosely woven material, such as the fish net weave, would be improper material. If you are uncertain, place your hand behind the material. If you can "see" your hand, find another article of clothing. When you are trying on slacks, notice whether you can see the edge of your undergarments through the material. If you can, find something else to wear. In addition, clothing that is tight or form fitting would not be modest. Many articles of athletic clothing, like those made out of spandex, hug the body so closely that you can easily see every detail of a woman's body. Very tight jeans can be a problem as well. Form fitting jeans can leave little doubt about what is underneath the pants.

Clothing that does not cover your nakedness is definitely not modest. However, clothing that does cover your sexual organs may still be considered immodest. For example, under the Old Law a man was not allowed wear women's clothing and a woman could not wear men's clothing (**Deuteronomy 22:5**). What is appropriate dress for a man and a woman varies greatly over time and between societies. Whatever is the current standard, that is the standard you must abide by.

Let's look at **I Timothy 2:9-10** again. The Greek word for modest is *kosmious*, which means orderly, well-arranged, seemly, or modest. In other words, "modest" refers to clothing that is neat and appropriate for the occasion. The Greek word that is translated shamefacedness is *aidos*, which means having a sense of shame, modesty, and reverence. A shamefaced person can blush when faced with things that are irreverent or immodest. The Greek word for sobriety is *sophrosuna*. This is a person of sound mind, with self-control, of good judgment, and moderate in all that he does.

Modest dress doesn't call attention to the wearer. This is a reason why clothing that exposes your nakedness is immodest. Costly jewelry or elaborate hair styles can also be immodest. People should notice a Christian because of who she is and not because of what she is wearing. Therefore, the clothing that I wear should fit the occasion so that my attire does not outshine my Lord, whom I represent. When going among farmers, you shouldn't wear a formal gown; a flannel shirt and jeans or a cotton dress would be more appropriate. If you need to teach someone of the Amish faith, you should wear a dark dress with no metal buttons.

For though I am free from all men, I have made myself a servant to all, that I might win the more; and to the Jews I became as a Jew, that I might win Jews; to those who are under the law, as under the law, that I might win those who are under the law; to those who are without law (not being without law toward God, but under law toward Christ), that I might win those who are without law; to the weak I became as weak, that I might win the weak. I have become all things to all men, that I might by all means save some. Now this I do for the gospel's sake, that I may be partaker of it with you. I Corinthians 9:19-23

We should always be modestly attired because we represent Jesus to those around us at every moment of our lives.

Before we leave the topic of clothing, I would like to mention one more thing. Right or wrong, people judge us by the clothes that we wear. If we dress as if we are going to dig ditches, but we are not, people will conclude that we don't care. If we greatly overdress for the occasion, people will conclude that we are stuck up and aloof. When you begin searching for a job, notice what the administrative people are wearing before you apply for the job. When you go in for an interview, dress at least as well as the person you will be talking to. When you are formally stopping by to teach the gospel, recognize that people have certain expectations about what a Christian should look like. Don't place a stumbling block in front of your message by dressing so that you lose credibility with people.

Hair Length

You may have difficulty believing this but God told us very plainly about how men and women ought to wear their hair. In **I Corinthians 11:14-15**, Paul tells us that it is natural for a man to wear short hair and for a woman to wear long hair. Short hair on a woman is a dishonor to that woman. The context of these verses shows that this is a statement of fact. It is not optional; it is not a suggestion; it is a fact that can be readily observed in the world.

If it is so natural, why do some women wear their hair short? The short hair is a symbol of their rebellion - rebellion against their parents, against society, against religion, or against everything. Until the feminist movement, women wore their hair long. When women rebelled against society, they cut their hair short. God is not pleased with people who rebel against things that are right. As Christians, we need to be more mature in our attitudes. Wrong things happen all the time in this world, but you cannot correct a wrong with another wrong.

Of course, the question then is how short is too short? **Deuteronomy 22:5** stated that clothing between men and women was to be distinctive. It seems reasonable that hair lengths between men and women should also be distinctive.

Questions

1)   Since fashions change constantly, how can we determine what is appropriate to wear?

2)   Using Genesis 2 and 3, what kind of clothing is definitely inadequate? What kind of clothing is definitely adequate?

3)   It is possible to be clothed and naked at the same time. Explain how this is so. List examples of this from current fashions.

4)   What is modest dress?

5)   Write out I Corinthians 11:14-15. What does it teach us?

Chapter 11
Rape

We must now discuss some of the less pleasant aspects of sex. Satan often takes things that are righteous before God and encourages man to pervert those acts into things that are wicked. Often men believe they have created something new, but sin has long existed in the world. As Solomon said, there is nothing new under the sun (**Ecclesiastes 1:9**).

Rape is when a man forces a woman to have sex with him. Instances of rape have been recorded in the Scriptures. It is consistently condemned by God. We have already read of the case of Shechem and Diana in **Genesis 34:1-7**. We will now turn to two other instances of rape that have been recorded in the Bible.

The first story we will read is in **Judges 19:22-28**.

Now as they were enjoying themselves, suddenly certain men of the city, perverted men, surrounded the house and beat on the door. They spoke to the master of the house, the old man, saying, "Bring out the man who came to your house, that we may know him carnally!" But the man, the master of the house, went out to them and said to them, "No, my brethren! I beg you, do not act so wickedly! Seeing this man has come into my house, do not commit this outrage. "Look, here is my virgin daughter and the man's concubine; let me bring them out now. Humble them, and do with them as you please; but to this man do not do such a vile thing!" But the men would not heed him. So the man took his concubine and brought her out to them. And they knew her and abused her all night until morning; and when the day began to break, they let her go. Then the woman came as the day was dawning, and fell down at the door of the man's house where her master was, till it was light. When her master arose in the morning, and opened the doors of the house and went out to go his way, there was his concubine, fallen at the door of the house with her hands on the threshold. And he said to her, "Get up and

let us be going." But there was no answer. So the man lifted her onto the donkey; and the man got up and went to his place.   Judges 19:22-28

[The phrase "that we may know him" means that they wanted to have sex with him. A virgin is someone who has never had sex before. To "humble" a woman in this context means to force her to have sex."They knew her and abused her" means they raped her. "There was no answer" because she was dead.]

A man of the tribe of Levi was traveling with his concubine. A concubine is a female servant who is married to her master. They stopped in the town of Gibeah to spend the night. That night, a group of men surrounded the house and began beating on the door. They insisted the Levite man come out of the house so that they could "know him." The phrase implies knowing a person very intimately. In other words, they wanted to have sex with him. You still hear the phrase "getting to know one another" as an indirect way of saying that someone had sex. Men having sex with men are called homosexuals. We will discuss the subject of homosexuals in the next chapter. For now, we will focus on the other events. The owner of the house, where the Levite was staying, tried to protect his guest by offering his daughter to the men. She had never had sex before, but the owner of the house said that these men could have sex with her. (Disgusting, isn't it?) The men would not hear of it. They wanted the guest instead, so the Levite sent his wife (concubine) out of the house. They raped her and abused her throughout the night. By morning, they let her go and she collapsed at the door of the house where they were staying. It was there that she died.

Why do you think this story is so repulsive? Why is rape a sin?

The second story is in **II Samuel 13:1-19**.

Now after this it was so that Absalom, the son of David had a lovely sister, whose name was Tamar; and Amnon the son of David loved her. Amnon was so distressed over his sister Tamar that he became sick; for she was a virgin. And it was improper for Amnon to do anything to her. But Amnon had a friend whose name was Jonadab the son of Shimeah, David's brother. Now Jonadab was a very crafty man. And he said to him, "Why are you, the king's son, becoming thinner day after day? Will you not tell me?" And Amnon said to him, "I love Tamar, my brother Absalom's sister." So Jonadab said to him, "Lie down on your bed and pretend to be ill. And when your father comes to see you, say to him, "Please let my sister Tamar come and give me food, and prepare the food in my sight, that I may see it and eat it from her hand."

Then Amnon lay down and pretended to be ill; and when the king came to see him, Amnon said to the king, "Please let Tamar my sister come and make a couple of cakes for me in my sight, that I may eat from her hand." And David sent home to Tamar, saying, "Now go to your brother Amnon's house, and prepare food for him." So Tamar went to her brother Amnon's house; and he was lying down. Then she took flour and kneaded it, made cakes in his sight, and baked the cakes. And she took the pan and placed them out before him, but he refused to eat. Then Amnon said, "Have everyone go out from me." And they all whet out from him. Then Amnon said to Tamar, "Bring the food into the bedroom, that I may eat from your hand." And Tamar took the cakes which she had made, and brought them to Amnon her brother in the bedroom.

Now when she had brought them to him to eat, he took hold of her and said to her, "Come, lie with me, my sister." And she answered him, "No, my brother, do not force me, for no such thing should be done in Israel. Do not do this disgraceful thing! And I, where could I take my shame? And as for you, you would be like one of the fools in Israel. Now therefore, please speak to the king; for he will not withhold me from you." However, he would not heed her voice; and being stronger than she, he forced her and lay with her.

Then Amnon hated her exceedingly, so that the hatred with which he hated her was greater than the love with which he had loved her. And Amnon said to her, "Arise, be gone!" And she said to him, "No, indeed! This evil of sending me away is worse than the other that you did to me." But he would not listen to her. Then he called his servant who attended him, and said, "Here! Put this woman out, away from me, and bolt the door behind her."

Now she had on a robe of many colors, for the king's virgin daughters wore such apparel. And his servant put her out and bolted the door behind her. Then Tamar put ashes on her head, and tore her robe of many colors that was on her, and laid her hand on her head and went away crying bitterly.

II Samuel 13:1-19

The story involves Amnon and Tamar. Amnon was Tamar's half-brother. King David was both Amnon and Tamar's father. However, Amnon and Tamar had different mothers. Tamar was very beautiful and Amnon thought that he was in love with her. He wanted to have sex with her, but he couldn't bring himself to do it because Tamar was a virgin. Under the Old Testament law, a man who raped an unmarried woman was required to marry her (**Exodus 22:16-17**). As we see from how the story ends, Amnon did not want to marry Tamar. He just wanted to have sex with her. He wanted it so badly that he was becoming ill. Unfortunately for everyone involved, Amnon had a crafty friend who suggested a way for Amnon to get Tamar alone. Perhaps Amnon thought he could get away with it if no one saw him raping his sister. Perhaps he thought he could convince Tamar not to tell anyone or that she would be so ashamed of what happened that she would not tell anyone about it.

Whatever the reason, Amnon played up his illness. His father asked if there was anything that he could do for his son. Amnon asked permission for Tamar to come to his house and prepare a meal for him. David, not suspecting anything, granted Amnon's wish and sent Tamar to his house. After preparing the meal, Amnon refused to eat until everyone left the house. He then asked Tamar to serve the meal in his bedroom. Once they were alone in the room, Amnon told Tamar that he wanted to have sex with her. Tamar refused. If Amnon wanted her so badly, he should have asked David for her hand in marriage. Tamar was certain David would have permitted it. However, as we already noted, Amnon was not interested in marriage. Because he was stronger than Tamar, he forced her into bed and raped her.

Once he satisfied his lust, he no longer wanted his sister. She told him that she should now live in his house as his wife. However, Amnon became enraged and had his servants throw her out of the house.

Do you think that Amnon truly loved his sister, or was he interpreting his lust for her as love? Many people continue to think that desiring to have sex with someone means that you are in love with that person. Such an idea is plainly false according to the Scriptures!

Who do you think is guilty of sin? Obviously, Amnon is guilty, but what about his crafty cousin, Jonadab? God said in **Romans 1:32**, that those who encourage others to sin are as deserving of death as those who actually commit the sinful act. Do you think Tamar also committed a sin? If you said yes, you are wrong. Throughout this story, Tamar tried to convince Amnon to abide by the Law of Moses. Even after the first sin, she still tried to make the best of a bad thing and marry the fool according to the Law. From all that we can see, Tamar did not want to break God's law and tried hard to resist Amnon. Amnon only won out because he was stronger than she.

Even though Tamar did not sin, it does not mean she did not act foolishly. Tamar had at least two advance warnings and possibly a third warning in advance of the actual rape. Since Amnon was lovesick over Tamar, it is possible that Tamar was aware of Amnon's feelings even if she did not realize how far Amnon would go to satisfy his desire. The second warning was when Amnon sent everyone out of the house. This is not normal behavior, and it was not wise for a young woman to stay alone in the house of a young man, even if he was ill. She should have insisted that others stay or that she would leave with the rest. Unfortunately, most of us do not want to think the worst of others, so we don't see the potential dangers ahead of us. The third warning was when Amnon asked Tamar into his bedroom when they were alone. If nothing else set off alarm bells, this one should have. The wise thing would have been for Tamar to run out of the house as Joseph did.

Young women, don't get caught in the trap of thinking that it can't happen to you. I was told of a sad tale of a young Christian girl who was asked over to a young man's house to celebrate his birthday. After the meal, his family all went out to the porch, but he kept her in the house, took her to his bedroom, and raped her. It is better to appear distrusting than to leave yourself open to forced sex. Your parents understand this. This is why they will insist that there are others around you.

Notice that in two of the three examples we looked at, the woman was raped by someone she knew. Recently the phrase "date rape" or "acquaintance rape" has been used to describe these situations. Statistically, about 20 percent of all rapes occur during a date. One estimate is that 80 percent of all rapes are done by someone known to the woman. Just because you are familiar with a man does not mean you should let your guard down.

Let us examine what the Law of Moses taught about rape. In **Exodus 22:16-17** and **Deuteronomy 22:28-29**, a situation is described where a man has sex with a woman who is unmarried, not engaged, and has not engaged in sex with anyone else. The act of sex between the couple could have been willingly done or unwillingly done. In either case, the man must pay the woman's father a dowry of 50 shekels of silver. A dowry is money or things given to the woman's parents for the privilege of marrying their daughter. The man was expected to marry the woman, unless the woman's father absolutely refused. In addition the man lost any rights to divorce his wife. Even if the father refused to allow his daughter to marry the man, the man still had to pay the dowry.

Where the woman is married or engaged to be married, the penalty is much more severe (**Deuteronomy 22:23-29**). In the times when the Bible was written, being engaged was considered nearly the same as being married. If the man raped the woman in an area where other people were nearby, it was assumed that the woman willingly had sex with the man since no one heard her cry out. In this case both the man and the woman were stoned to death. If the rape took place where it was unlikely anyone would have heard the woman scream, the man was stoned but the woman was presumed to be innocent of any sin.

A woman has not committed a sin just because she was raped. Unfortunately, many people don't seem to understand this. Too often people assume that the woman must have enticed the man in some way. If not directly, then by the way she dressed or by the way she moved. Imagine that you just had your bike stolen and a friend of yours walks up to you:

"Someone stole your bike. Too bad. You really ought to have been more careful.

Serves you right, leaving your bike out
where a person couldn't help but want to
steal it."

"What do you mean? I locked my bike before
I went to class. They cut the chain with a
bolt cutter."

"Sure. Even if you did remember to lock it,
why did you leave your brand-new bike out
in front of the building where everyone could
see it?"

Do you see how this "friend" is implying that you are guilty
of some undefined sin because you had a bike stolen? The
same thing happens when a woman is accused of leading a
man on. It doesn't matter what she did or did not do from
the man's perspective. The man still had sex with a woman
with whom he was not married! No matter how you look at
it, the man is guilty of sin. Being led into sin doesn't lessen
his guilt one bit. If the woman willingly had sex with the
man, then she too is guilty of sexual immorality. However, if
she resisted to the best of her ability, then she is innocent
before God.

Recently, some women have tried to redefine rape as
any time a woman has sex and the woman did not want it at
that time. This is an inaccurate definition by God's standard.
In a marriage, a woman is never to withhold sexual
privileges from her husband; just as a man must always be
ready to satisfy his wife's desire for sex (**I Corinthians 7:2-
5**). From the Bible's perspective, it is not possible for a
husband to rape his own wife.

Questions

1)   What did Shechem do with Diana in Genesis 34:1-7
        that was wrong? Why was it wrong?

2)   What did the men of Gibeah in Judges 19:22-28 do
        to the Levite's wife that was wrong? Why was it
        wrong?

3)   What did Amnon do to Tamar in II Samuel 13:1-19
        that was wrong? Why was it wrong?

4)   In Shechem's and Amnon's cases, what would have
        been the correct thing to do?

5)   Is a woman guilty of some sin when she is raped?
        Why or why not?

6)   In the story of Amnon and Tamar, what was
        Jonadab's sin?

Chapter 12
Other Sexual Perversions

Homosexuality

A homosexual is a person who has sexual relations with another person of the same sex. A man having sex with a man is a homosexual. A woman having sex with a woman is also a homosexual, though many people use the term lesbian for a female homosexual. Unlike what you may have been taught in school and what you have seen on television, God teaches us that homosexuality is not due to a genetic difference. People are not born with a predisposition toward wanting to have sex with someone of their own sex; nor does God consider homosexuality an acceptable alternative lifestyle. To God, homosexuality is a sin - nothing more and nothing less.

People want to say that there is a genetic disposition toward homosexuality to remove from themselves any blame for their actions. If people were born homosexuals, it would be difficult to claim that it is a sin. If people can't help being homosexual, then God would be unfair to label their actions as wrongful. Similarly, to call living in a homosexual relationship an alternative lifestyle is an attempt to get society as a whole to view homosexuality as normal, everyday behavior.

The Bible is very explicit about God's opinion on homosexuality. In the Old Testament there is a law recorded in **Leviticus 18:22** that clearly says a man is not to have sex with another man. People who were guilty of such acts were punished by death (**Leviticus 20:13**). The New Testament is also clear on the topic of homosexuality. In **Romans 1:24-32**, Paul describes the moral decay of the Gentile people over the years. The people turned their backs on

God, so God gave up on them and allowed them to practice
what their hearts desired. The first phase was the
committing of sexual sins such as fornication and adultery.
They worshiped the body instead of the Creator of man.
The second phase was when women began having sexual
relations with women. Paul described it as exchanging the
natural use of the body (having sex with a man) for an
unnatural use. It is obvious from the way God created men
and women that men were not designed to have sex with
men, and women were not designed to have sex with
women. As a result, these people burned in their lusts for
one another and committed acts that are shameful. The
result is that the acts carry the penalties for the actions.
Homosexuals are plagued with diseases that are only
transmitted sexually. While these diseases are not the final
punishment, they serve as a warning of the punishment to
come. Unfortunately, it doesn't stop there. People who want
nothing to do with God have nothing to stop them from
committing any number of sins. However, the people who
commit these sins will face an eternity in Hell. Not only the
people who actually commit the sins, but also the people
who approve of the deeds though they don't participate in
them.

  You cannot be a homosexual and be a faithful
member of the church. However, the church does contain
people who had committed homosexual acts before they
learned the truth and turned to the Lord (**I Corinthians
6:9-11**). Baptism can wash away all sins, if we will just turn
our lives around and live righteously before the Lord.
Baptism does not make homosexuality acceptable. A person
wanting to be a child of God must give up his sinful
practices. A thief cannot continue to steal after becoming a

Christian, nor can a lesbian continue to have sexual relations with a woman after becoming a child of God.

Sometimes you will hear people claim that the Bible doesn't condemn homosexuality. Obviously, the verses we have just read show this claim to be false. The idea that the Bible doesn't condemn homosexuality is derived from the fact that the King James Version of the Bible does not contain the word homosexual. That statement is true. When the King James Version was written in 1611, the English

language did not include a specific word for the act of a woman having sex with a woman. However, it doesn't mean that the Bible does not talk about the idea, nor does it mean that God doesn't condemn the act. Modern English does contain the word homosexuality. You will find that the new English versions, such as the New King James and the New International Version, use the word homosexual in the appropriate places.

Many people believe that homosexuality is a relatively new phenomenon. It isn't. People have been guilty of homosexual acts from as early as the days of Abraham, if not earlier. In **Genesis 19:1-25**, we have the account of the destruction of Sodom and Gomorrah. These towns were very wicked. When two men (who were actually angels) entered the city, Lot insisted that they spend the night at his house. After supper, the men of the city, young and old alike, surrounded Lot's house. They told Lot to send the strangers out so that they could have sex with them. ("To have sex" is the meaning of the phrase "that we may know them.") Lot went out and tried to strike a deal with the men. He offered to send out his two virgin daughters. They could do whatever they liked with them, but they could not have his guests. The men rejected the idea and threatened to do worse things to Lot than they would have done to the men. At the last moment, the angels rescued Lot by striking the men with blindness.

In **Judges 19:16-28**, we read of an account that is similar to what happened in Sodom. As in the earlier account, some men of the city of Gibeah surrounded the house where a stranger was spending the night. They demanded that the owner of the house send out the stranger so that they could "know him." In other words, they wanted to have sex with the man. Once again, they refused the offer of an exchange of a woman for the man. However, when a woman was all they could get their hands on, they raped her all night.

The word "sodomy" was derived from the name of the town famous for its homosexuals. The word means a male prostitute (a man who will hire himself out for sex). It especially means a homosexual. In recent years, the meaning of the word sodomy has broadened to refer to any sexual act that doesn't include copulation (the man's penis entering the woman's vagina). The following verses show that homosexuality was a continuing problem in Israel: **I Kings 14:24, I Kings 15:12, I Kings 22:46**, and **II Kings 23:7**.

Some women talk themselves into believing they are "naturally" homosexuals because they find other women arousing. We talked about arousal early in this book and showed that after you reach puberty, arousal is a physical response to physical or mental stimulation. Over time this response becomes more refined. Eventually it will be focused on men, and one day you will learn to focus all your desires on your husband. However, somewhere along the way, some women focus on other women instead of men. This can be corrected with conscious effort on the woman's part, but too many people these days have no desire to learn to live righteously. Instead, they seek out other women who have similar lusts and begin stimulating each other to higher and higher sexual desires.

Anyone can arouse the sexual desires within you, man or woman. Arousal and the desire for sex are physical responses to things like sights, sounds, and, most of all, touch. Just because a woman manages to arouse the desire for sex within you does not mean you have to give in to that desire. Remember Satan uses our own desires to lead us into situations where it looks like the only way to satisfy those desires is to sin. Don't be deceived by Satan! If nothing else, walk away from the temptation. Just don't give in to sin!

It is obvious from the way God designed the sexual organs of men and women that sex is to be between members of the opposite sexes. We don't even have to turn to a Scripture to prove this. It is obvious from a natural viewpoint. Homosexuality is not a natural phenomenon. It is something that men and women decide to do that is against nature. Yes, the women that participate in it most likely enjoy what they are doing. I'm sure some people get a thrill out of stealing and murdering as well. However, fun doesn't make an action right or wrong. God views women having sex with other women as an abomination. (An abomination is something extremely disgusting and repulsive.)

Sex is pleasurable, but restrict yourself to enjoying sex God's way - with your husband.

Incest

When a person has sex with other members of his own family, it is called incest. In **Leviticus 18:6-18,** God gives a long list of various relationships that he does not consider righteous. The idea of uncovering a person's nakedness implies more than just happening to see a person without clothing. The wording is such that we are talking about a person removing someone's clothing to expose their genitals. It is implied that the purpose of this is to have sex with that person. Notice that uncovering a man's wife is equated to uncovering the man himself. The only person who should have sex with a woman is her husband. Any violation of that is a violation of the husband as well as the wife.

Leviticus 20:11-12,17-21 gives the punishments for having sexual relationships with a close relative. A man who had sex with his mother, stepmother, daughter-in-law, or stepdaughter is punished by death. The woman who consented to have sex with him was also put to death. Other sexual relationships with family members were punished by exiling the guilty couple. The couple were no longer considered Israelites.

Obviously, incest has been a problem for a long time in the world. Among the many other problems that Israel had, they were guilty of incest (**Ezekiel 22:10-11**). Even the early church faced this problem. In **I Corinthians 5:1-5**, we are told that a member of the church at Corinth was living with his father's wife. Instead of being appalled by this sin, as even non-Christians would have been, the Corinthian Christians were proud to have this man among them. Paul severely scolded them for their sinful pride and demanded that they immediately separate themselves from this sinful man.

In the passages that we have considered, there is an implication that the people involved in the incest were old enough to desire sex and had consented to the act. Sometimes children are forced to have sex by another member of their family. While we could label this incest, it would also be called rape. Just as a woman who was raped by a man is not guilty of sin, neither is a child guilty of sin when forced to have sex with someone else.

Bestiality

Bestiality means having sex with animals. I am sure you find the very thought disgusting and difficult to imagine. However, believe me, if there is a way to pervert God's creation someone somewhere has figured out a way to do it.

God clearly condemns the practice in **Leviticus 18:23**. The punishment was death for both the human and the animal involved (**Exodus 22:19; Leviticus 20:15-16**).

Questions

1) List three verses that prove homosexuality is a sin.

2) How else do we know that homosexuality is not natural?

3) How long has homosexuality been around? When is it first mentioned in the Scriptures?

4) What is incest?

5) What does it mean to uncover a person's nakedness?

6) If a child is forced to have sex with an adult, who is guilty of sin?

7) What is bestiality?

Chapter 13
Prostitution

Because sex is pleasurable, it isn't surprising that there are people who try to make money with it. People who sell themselves to other people for sex are called prostitutes. Other terms used in the Bible for these people are harlot and whore. While most prostitutes are selling sex for money, some prostitutes use sex to gain favors. Prostitutes can be male or female (see **Deuteronomy 23:17-18**), young or old.

People who engage in prostitution have taken an act that expresses the bond between a man and a woman in a committed relationship and have lowered it to the level of animals. Most animals will mate in response to instincts. They do not require love and commitment before they have sex. This is why male prostitutes are referred to as dogs in **Deuteronomy 23:17-18.** In **Jeremiah 13:27**, the city of Jerusalem's unfaithfulness to God is compared to the willingness of a prostitute to take in any man. The prostitutes in turn are compared to horses loudly neighing their desire to mate in the fields. Men who use the services of a prostitute are also compared to lustful stallions pursuing mares (**Jeremiah 5:7-8**). Judah's strong desire to worship idols and make treaties with foreign nations is compared to a woman looking to have sex with men with large genitals (**Ezekiel 23:20**). The men's sexual organs are compared to donkeys and horses.

All of this shows the degradation of the beauty of human sex within a marriage to raw animalistic intercourse. This is one of the reasons Dinah's brothers were upset with Shechem. His treatment of Dinah was no better than a man using the services of a prostitute (**Genesis 34:31**). He may have come to love her afterwards, but he had treated her no better than an animal.

The primary excuse for engaging in prostitution is the money that is paid (**Hosea 2:2-7, 9:1**). However, some are prostitutes because they desire sex. The nation of Israel was compared to a woman who lusting after young men, allowed them to fondle her breasts and have sex with her (**Ezekiel 23:5-10**). Israel was eventually destroyed for her sins. Rather than learning from the fall of her sister nation, Judah also takes up the life of a harlot. If anything, she behaves even worse than Israel, hotly pursuing any young stud she fancied (**Ezekiel 23:11-21**). Both of these reasons are poor excuses for a lack of self-control.

Prostitution not only violates the laws of God, it also brings danger to those engaging in it. Since prostitutes often have multiple partners, and those partners often have sex with multiple partners, diseases spread quickly among these people. For this reason, harlotry is called an unclean practice (**Psalm 106:39**). These diseases will shorten the life of those engaging in prostitution (**Job 36:14**). Even with today's modern medicines, most promiscuous people die young. We are unable to prevent all the damage caused by sexually transmitted diseases.

However, there is a more hidden danger to prostitution. Anytime a man or a woman engages in sex, there is a physical uniting of the two bodies and there is an emotional uniting of the two souls (**I Corinthians 6:15-20**). Since prostitutes bond with many men, they become calloused and are unable to form a relationship if they ever try to get married. Think about it this way: Take two pieces of duct tape and put the sticky sides together. It is nearly impossible to pull them apart. However, take two more pieces of tape and start sticking them to other things (the chair, the floor, your clothes, etc.). Now when you put them together, they easily separate. The tape was soiled by its previous contacts. The same thing happens when men and women soil themselves with uncommitted sex.

Even though the danger is real, prostitutes ignore it. They don't believe they have done anything wrong (**Proverbs 30:20**). For this reason they are called simple-minded (**Proverbs 9:13**). Harlotry, like alcoholic drinks, takes away the reasoning ability of those who use it (**Hosea 4:11**). Her soul is in danger, she is walking the path to Hell, and she doesn't even know it (**Proverbs 5:5-6**).

All prostitution is not just for money. Some women engage in it for favors. A woman may decide to have sex with her boss so he will favor her in a future promotion. Others use it as a way of gaining power over men. Some foolish girls think that allowing a boy to have sex with her will keep him by her. All of these are just other forms of harlotry. The man involved is just getting sexual gratification and he doesn't even have to pay for it. The relationship has decayed to one of animalistic desire, and like an animal, the man will easily leave to find new places to relieve his desires.

It is foolish to have sex with anyone who is not your husband. Therefore it would be wise to avoid the behavior of those who sell themselves for sex. While fashions change, there have always been styles of clothing that advertise a woman is a prostitute. At one point it was the wearing of a veil (**Genesis 38:13-26**). It could be other things (see **Proverbs 7:1-27** and note verse 10). Prostitutes also advertise themselves by certain behaviors. In **Song of Solomon 1:7-8**, the young woman wanted to know when was the best time to meet Solomon on his lunch break. She did not want to wander aimlessly on the hills, approaching different shepherds as if she was a harlot. Instead of helping her, the ladies of the court tell her she should do just that and make sure she leads a goat along too. A goat was considered the standard payment for the service of a prostitute, so a woman leading goats was advertising her trade. In Paul's days prostitutes wore their hair very short (**I Corinthians 11:6**) – probably to cut down on lice.

Don't flaunt your beauty and your finery like a harlot looking for customers (**Ezekiel 16:15-16; Proverbs 6:25**). Do not act brazenly around men (**Proverbs 7:11, 13**) or they may mistake your intentions. And obviously, don't allow men to fondle you (**Ezekiel 23:3**). Yes, a man is wrong to be looking for sex outside the realm of marriage, but it is also wrong to advertise your willingness to engage in sex, whether intentionally or not.

Consider this article written by high school educator Elizabeth Schuett.

> Sally's standing in front of my desk, tugging at her painted-on mini skirt, the one that's smaller than my favorite dishtowel, and complaining. "Arthur is sexually harassing me."
> I hate it when that happens.
> Occasionally, I regret encouraging 14-year-olds to read. Too many seem to think Grandma's grocery store tabloid is the Midwest equivalent of The Wall Street Journal.
> But I'm obliged to investigate. "What has Arthur done?"
> "He looks at my legs." I try not to splutter or roll my eyes. Objectivity is my job. "He said my skirt was too short."

I encourage her to get on to the harassment part. She says that's it.

We have a dress code where I teach, and most of our kids come to school looking just fine. Of course, there are a couple of guys who have bought into what someone has told them is the gang look. They come to school dressed like derelicts with their outsized pants dragging the floor.

Kind of makes you wonder if their mothers watch them going out the door looking like that or if the kid is changing clothes in the alley, stashing his Levis in a handy hedge.

They want to wear their ball caps turned around backwards because they think it makes them look "really bad" and continually test and protest the school rule of no hats in the building.

Sally's skirt is too short. And it's too tight. I ask her if it's comfortable.

"Oh sure. It's great."

"Then why are you constantly tugging at it?"

Are you ready for the answer? "Because that's what they do in the movies. Guys like it." Being an educator is an education.

"Then maybe Arthur was doing exactly what you wanted him to do," I suggested.

You know what she says? She says it wasn't Arthur's attention she was trying to attract.

I explain to her that virtual nudity is not selective and if she's going to go around with her backside hanging out she'll have to learn to deal with unprogrammed responses.

Sally says I ought to do something about Arthur. I ask her what she would suggest. Paint his eyeballs black and buy him a guide dog?

Sally's not too happy with my lack of sympathy and informs me, rather shortly, that her mother *encourages* her expressions of individuality. I suggest her search for singularity is going to land her in the pneumonia ward.

Sally demands to know what I'm going to do about Arthur. I tell her nothing. I ask what she's going to do about her skirt. She says she's going to tell her mother on me.

Sure, why not? I'm thinking. Briefly, the question crosses my mind: Is this what I went to college for? So I can explain to somebody's out-to-lunch mother why her daughter, the one with her fanny fanning the breeze, has no harassment case?

If there's a victim here, it's Arthur. He's got hormones, too, you know.

The problem as I see it, is the simple fact that I'm not Sally's parent. I'm her teacher. It *is* my responsibility to see to it that Sally can read, write, and enjoy literature. I'm professionally bound to introduce Sally to three-point, five-paragraph essays and descriptive writing. Compare, contrast, write a letter to the editor; that's what I do, and I feel twice blessed if I can help her enjoy it along the way.

However, it is *not* my job to have to explain to a grown woman why her teenage daughter should not come to school wearing clothes that would be more appropriate on a street hooker.

I'd like to let her know the injustice she's doing her daughter by not only allowing such absurd behavior but encouraging it and then, when the outcome doesn't meet expectations, blaming it all on Arthur. I'd like to accuse her of depriving her daughter of a childhood and causing a 14-year-old to make grownup decisions.

But most of all, I guess I'm curious to know why she's willing to sit back and let someone else raise her child.

Questions

1)   What is a prostitute?

2)   How does a prostitute attract customers?

3)   How can you avoid appearing to be a prostitute?

4)   Why do some women engage in prostitution?

5)   Fornication is not only a sin against God, it is also a sin against whom?

6)   What are the physical consequences of being a prostitute?

7)   Recall the man who let men rape his wife in Judges 19. While not excusing his sin, what caused him to lose his affection for his wife (see Judges 19:2)?

Appendix A
A Note to Parents and Teachers

It may be tempting to just give this book to your teenager and say, "Here, read this." However, unless your teenager is different from those I know, it won't work. The book will never be read. After all, a grown-up thinks this is good for her, and we all know how boring other "good for you" books like Shakespeare and Longfellow turned out to be. Another bad tactic is to stress how much the book will teach her about things she doesn't already know. Most teenagers are inflicted with the disease of thinking they know everything. Reading the book would be admitting that they don't know everything about sex. I strongly recommend sitting down for an hour or so a day and studying the material with your child. This is the only way you can guarantee that the Scriptures are read and understood. If you insist on having your child study the material on her own, the best suggestion that I have heard is to sit down in the evenings and read the material where your daughter can see you, and then leave the book out on the coffee table. After a few days, her curiosity will lead her to look inside, and I hope the book will be interesting enough to hold her attention. Don't mention the book until you know she has been reading it for a few days. I would then suggest asking what happened to the book and begin talking to her about the contents.

I have a few suggestions for using this book as part of a class, whether in church or at home with your own children. When the girls have reached puberty, around the age of 12 for most children, place them in a separate class to teach them this material. Both the students and the teacher will find the material in this book embarrassing – too embarrassing to talk about in detail if men are a part of the class. Another series is available that addresses the same topics and Scriptures from the male point of view. Please use the other series in a separate class for the boys when they reach puberty.

The material in this book assumes that the girls have already reached puberty. This book will answer many questions every girl has when she finds out she is changing into a woman.

I urge you not to postpone the material too long. The public school system, television shows, and peers will be teaching the girls many things that would be best to straighten out early. We also know that many children begin experimenting with sex shortly after they are capable. Rutger's University's National Marriage Project issued a report on July 1, 1999. One finding they gave was that over half of teenage girls have had sexual intercourse by the age of 17. Even more disturbing is that these numbers have risen rapidly over the years. Attitudes towards sexual sins are also dramatically changing. The percentage of teenage girls who said having a child out of wedlock is a "worthwhile lifestyle" grew from 33 percent to 53 percent during the 1970's and 1980's. It is better to prevent a sin than to restore someone from that sin.

When teaching the material, have the students take turns reading each passage aloud. Don't trust that these verses will be read at home. After each reading, explain the meaning of the phrases that may be confusing to the students. Most girls don't recognize the terminology dealing with sex; they have just become fully aware that sex exists and is relevant to them.

Don't count on long class discussions. If you think this material is embarrassing, the girls will find it even more so. You will find that the students will tend to answer direct questions in as few words as possible. Although you encourage the girls to ask any question that they may have, and you give them frequent opportunities to ask those questions, they may be too embarrassed to put their questions in verbal form. Watch their body language to see if they understand the material.

Appendix B
Contacting the Author

I realize that talking about sex with young women is very difficult. It doesn't matter whether they are your own children or members of your congregation; the subject is just a little too personal. However, I feel very strongly that these things must be discussed and taught to every young woman. Just because a girl's body is changing into a woman's body does not mean that she will automatically acquire all sorts of knowledge about what is happening to her, whether it is normal or not, or how to behave with her newly developed abilities.

If, after going over this material, you find you are still uncomfortable with the idea of teaching the material to your girls, please feel free to contact me.

If you have <u>any</u> questions about the topics covered in this book, feel free to write to me. I will answer the question as accurately and frankly as I can. I will keep all correspondence confidential.

You can reach me via email at <u>minister@lavistachurchofchrist.org</u>

Appendix C
Selected Answers to Questions

Since writing the initial *Growing Up in the Lord* books for both boys and girls, I have placed the material on the Internet (at http://lavistachurchofchrist.org). As a result I have had a large number of teenagers write with questions. I've selected a few of them to place in this edition so you can see the kinds of questions other teenagers are asking.

> I am 11 years and 8 months old. I also have a moderate amount of acne. What can be done about it?

Acne is a pain during the teenage years. The only comfort is that it will fade once you have grown (though it may not completely go away). Acne is caused by three factors: your growing skin produces more oils during growth, your skin is shedding dead cells at a faster rate, and bacteria love the free food. The oils and skin cells tend to plug the oil glands, which then swell and look ugly. Bacteria get trapped under the plug and and have a free for all, which causes you skin to swell and redden as your body tries to battle the bacteria. There are three basic products to help the situation:

1.   Soap is the first line of defense. It removes excess oil and skin cells, and it kills off a lot of bacteria. So keeping your skin washed will help a lot. The problem is that it is hard to control how much oil you are removing and it can cause the skin to become overly dry.

2.   Cleansing products with salicylic acid or glycolic acid soften and helps remove excess skin cells.

Fewer free skin cells means fewer clogs. Many people, however, find these mild acids to be irritating. Instead of using it everywhere, it is better to use it in spots where the acne is worse.

3.   Products containing benzoyl peroxide kill bacteria on the surface of your skin. While it can't stop the plugs, it can keep them from getting red and swollen. You can find it in a 2.5% and a 10% solution. The 2.5% is actually adequate. Many people find the 10% solution irritating to their skin.

Generally you will have to experiment to figure out how much, how often, and where you need various products to get a good result. Once your periods start, you will have to make alterations as the fluctuating hormones of your monthly cycle will change what you need and when you need them.

> How do you know if your breasts have finished
> developing?

For the average girl, your breasts will reach their
adult size and shape about four years after your first
menarche (your first period). Generally this is reached by
the time most girls are seventeen or eighteen -- age fifteen is
the average age to reach your full adult height and shape.

Doctor Tanner developed a system to determine
how far a child has progressed during adolescence. They are
called the Tanner Stages.

1. Stage one is your shape during childhood. Your
    chest is flat and you have no pubic hair.

2. In stage two, your breasts begin to bud. The nipples
    swell and the breasts are tender to the touch. The
    areola (the dark area around your nipples) begins to
    widen. Sparse, fine hair appears on your labia
    majora (the groin area between your legs).

3. During stage three, your milk producing glands
    begin to develop and the fat needed to support milk
    production is laid down in the breasts. This causes
    the breasts to swell in size so that if you look at
    yourself in the mirror straight on, the breasts extend
    beyond the rim of the areola. Your pubic hair
    becomes curly and coarser in texture. The hair
    begins to fill in the groin area so that it vaguely
    resembles an upside-down triangle.

4. In stage four, the breasts change shape, though the
    size remains roughly the same. Your nipples
    distinctly protrude and the area of the areola and
    nipple form a secondary mound on top of the mound
    of the breast. A girl's first menarche (period) is

usually, but not always, experienced in this stage, but the menarches are not usually regular. The pubic hair forms a full triangle, but doesn't yet extend to the thighs. Underarm hair begins to form during this stage as well.

5.   Stage five is your full adult shape. You should be experiencing almost regular menarche. The areola is now shaped with the rest of the breast and only the nipples protrude. Your pubic hair extends a bit to the inner thighs.

By judging which stage you are in, you can determine how much further your breasts will grow. To estimate what stage of development you are in, see the Tanner Stage Calculator for Girls at http://lavistachurchofchrist.org/LVstudies/GrowingUpInThe Lord/Girls/TannerStage.htm.

> I am 14 years old, female, and my left breast is larger than the other, including the nipple and the area around the nipple. Is it normal? Please tell me. I am really worried.

Development does not always happen in a perfectly symmetrical fashion. It is not unusual for one side to get ahead of the other side for a short period of time. It will soon balance out as the other side catches up.

> I am 12 and a half years old. I recently got my periods.
> My sister says that after you get periods you stop
> growing in height. Is that true?

Some girls get their first period during stage 2,
others get it during stage 4. It is the latter group that leads
to the idea that you stop growing after you have your
menstrual period because the next stage is 5 when all
growth stops. But this is not true in all cases. Since you are
most likely in stage 2, you will still have your major growth
spurt (which happens in stage 3).

> Will a girl gain weight before menstruation?

If you are asking if weight gain is common before a
girl's first menstruation cycle (the first period is called
menarche), the answer is "yes." Menarche is one of the
earlier signs that a girl is in her adolescent years. About the
time of puberty, your body begins to store up extra fat to
help fuel the many changes that takes place during
adolescence. This excess fat is usually used up when you go
through your growth spurt.

Once you begin experiencing a monthly
menstruation cycle, you will also notice a gain in weight just
prior to your periods. The gain is temporary and is due to
water retention caused by the shifting hormones in your
body. The same shift in hormones might cause other
symptoms, such as a craving for sweets, headaches, fatigue,
or even grouchiness. Fortunately these symptoms only last a
few days to a week at a time.

I am very thin and my periods don't come regularly. Why is it so important to eat right to have regular periods? What will happen if you don't?

A woman's body is designed to be able to bear children. However, there is a danger of being pregnant when not enough food is available. Since the growing child need nutrients, the body would be forced to "steal" from the mother's body in order to support the child. God designed the woman's body to hinder this situation. When you don't have the minimum reserves to support a developing child, the body stops the menstrual cycles -- no menstrual cycles, no baby will be produced.

There have been studies on women athletes that show that a few months in a row with no periods begins a loss in bone strength. Whether this extends to non-athletes without periods is currently not known. But loss in bone strength can be permanent, so it is not worth the risk.

Periods during your teenage years will be irregular anyway. But if you are not eating enough to maintain a regular period, then you are probably not getting enough nutrition for other vital parts of your body. Especially during your years of growth, a lack of proper nutrition will impact your growth.

> Can a best friend, who says he only likes me as a friend, possibly be hiding his feelings for me?

Most men are relatively simple creatures. I know it, being one myself. We like to solve problems. We like to go straight to the answer with as little fuss as possible. It is the directness of men that causes many of the misunderstandings between men and women.

Women tend to over-analyze men. Oh sure, they hear what we say, but they are certain that we can't really mean it that way. There *must* be something more to it than that! Odd thing is that there rarely is anything more to it.

Therefore, any woman needs to be careful that she is not reading what she wishes were true into a situation. Let's look at your friend's statement:

1.   He really likes you as a friend, but he is not willing to think of you as his future wife. He is a true friend because he is telling you just the way it is. He is not leading you on with false hopes.

2.   He is not ready to make a commitment to any woman, even though he truly likes your friendship. He is being honest with you because of that friendship. He doesn't want to tie you down to him since he doesn't know when he will become more serious about marriage.

3.   He is madly in love with you, but he doesn't want you to know, so he is willing to lie to you to keep his feelings hidden. But since he is willing to lie, this must mean he really doesn't think much of you.

Regardless of your feelings, look at this and tell me which of these scenarios is more plausible? Your feelings lead you to #3, but your intellect says that it leads to a self-contradiction in character.

Think carefully about this: If he is telling you a lie ("we're only friends") and you believe it is not true, why are you seeking someone who is willing to lie to you? Why do you want someone whom you basically said you can't trust to say what he means?

> *"Faithful are the wounds of a friend, but the kisses of an enemy are deceitful"* (Proverbs 27:6).

I am twelve years old. My crush's birthday is the day after mine. He is always saying he only likes me as a friend, but I told him that I liked him as more than just a friend. I like him a lot; I just don't want to ruin our friendship. He said it was cool because we are such good friends. Should I ask him out and see what happens or should I just wait?

[The following came the next day.]

My friend told me why he didn't want to date me now. It's because he is afraid that we may break-up and not be friends any more. Does that mean he really doesn't want to date me any more? Or maybe he just really likes me. Do you think he likes me or what?

Let's try to look at this from a practical viewpoint. In most states, you will not be able to marry until you're eighteen. So you are looking at a minimum of a six year relationship. Now think about the things you liked six years ago. (I know that was half your life ago, but this will make a significant point.) What were your favorite shows, foods, and activities? I suspect that your current favorites are drastically different today than they were six years ago.

At your current age, you are in a period of life where you are changing just as rapidly as you did from the time you were in kindergarten. Just as the things that you like then are different from today, so will be the things you like six years from now will be different.

It appears your friend understands this. It is good to have friends, but twelve is too early to think about commitments. Of course he likes you! He has said it. But I feel sorry for him because you don't believe him. You are wanting more from him than he is willing to give at this moment in time. You really ought to respect him by accepting what he has said.

Be friends. Do things together. Laugh and have fun. *"Rejoice, O young man, in your youth, and let your heart cheer you in the days of your youth; walk in the ways of your heart, and in the sight of your eyes; but know that for all these God will bring you into judgment"* (Ecclesiastes 11:9). If there is something there to build a permanent relationship upon, it will grow. If not, it will die off. All the pushing and prodding that you do will not change it one bit. Asking your friend out on a date won't make him like you more or less. Rushing life won't make it more pleasant.

"Let your conduct be without covetousness; be content with such things as you have ..." (Hebrews 13:5). The word "covetousness" means being greedy for something more. Life will be more pleasant if you learn to be happy with the way things are instead pushing to make things the way you think they ought to be. And it will close the door on a path Satan will use against you, to tempt you to go farther than you ought.

Glossary

acne (AK-nê) Pimples on the skin caused by blocked oil glands.

adolescence (ad-ôl-ESS-enc) The years during which a person is rapidly changing from a child to an adult.

arousal (a-ROUZ-al) The desire for sex.

clitoris (KLIT-o-ris) A part of the female body that gives pleasurable feelings during intercourse. The clitoris is located just inside the vulva.

coitus (KÔ-it-us) That portion of sexual intercourse when a man's penis is within a woman's vagina.

condom (KON-dom) A stretchable bag that fits over the male penis to capture semen.

douche (DOOSH) A liquid squirted into the vagina for the purpose of cleansing it.

ejaculate (ê-JACK-û-lât) Semen that is ejected from the male penis which contains sperm.

ejaculation (ê-JACK-û-lâ-shun) The act of ejecting semen.

estrogens (ES-tro-jens) Female hormones that regulate the reproductive system.

fornication (for-ni-KÂ-shun) Sexual intercourse other than between a husband and wife.

foreplay (FOR-play) The fondling, touching, and caressing of the body in sexual ways to prepare for intercourse.

genitals (GEN-it-als) The organs of the body related to sex.

harlot (HAR-lot) A woman who offers sex in exchange for money or favors.

homosexual (hô-mô-SEX-û-al) A person who desires to have sex with a person of the same sex.

hormone (HOR-môn) A chemical produced by the body which affects the activity of cells in the body.

hymen (HI-men) A partial covering of skin over the entrance of the vagina.

incest (IN-sest) Sexual intercourse between close relatives.

infatuation (in-FACH-u-a-shun) Love for what you imagine a person to be.

lasciviousness (la-SIV-ê-us-nes) Being lewd or lustful.

lesbian (LEZ-bê-an) A woman who engages in sex with another woman.

licentiousness (lî-SEN-chus-nes) Lacking sexual restraint.

lust (LUST) Strong desires, in particular, a strong desire to do what is sinful.

masturbation (MAS-tur-ba-shun) Fondling of oneself to create sexual feelings, usually to the point of orgasm.

orgasm (ÔR-gaz-im) The height of sexual excitement.

ovaries (O-va-rees) The female organ that holds eggs and is the primary source of estrogens.

penis (PEE-nis) A part of the male external sex organs. It is also a part of the male's urinary system.

pregnancy (PREG-nan-cee) When an egg is fertilized with a male sperm and implants itself in the lining of the uterus.

prostitute (PROS-ti-TÛT) One who indiscriminately engages in sex, especially for money.

puberty (PÛ-ber-tê) The time when a child begins changing into an adult.

sperm (SPERM) The male half of the two things that must be combined to produce a child. (The female half is called an egg.) Sperm is sometimes called seed in the Bible.

uterus (U-ter-us) The organ designed to carry a child when a woman is pregnant.

vagina (va-GÎ-na) The canal that connects the female's uterus and the external opening.

vulva (VUL-va) The opening to the vagina.

whore (WÔR) A prostitute.

womb (WHOOM) Another name for the uterus.

Index